THE GOSPEL OF THOMAS

ⲧⲉⲛ̣ϩⲉ̣ⲉⲧⲓ̈ⲙⲙⲁⲩⲁ̣ⲩⲱⲧ̣ⲁ̣
ⲧⲁⲧⲟⲟⲩⲥⲁⲩⲉⲓⲉϥ· ⲕⲁ̣ⲩ̣ⲁ̣ ⲁⲡⲉⲧⲟⲙ̣
ⲁⲣⲭⲏ ⲛ̅ϯⲅⲟⲙ̅ⲧⲉⲧ̅ⲙ̅ⲛ̅ⲉⲣ ⲡⲟⲩⲃⲏ̣ⲩ̣
ⲡⲉϫⲉⲓ̅ⲥ̅ ϫⲉⲡⲉⲛⲧⲁ̅ϭ̅ⲓⲛⲉ̣ ⲙ̅ⲕⲟⲥⲙⲟⲥ
ⲛ̅ϥ̅ⲣ̅ⲣ̅ⲙⲙⲁⲟ ⲙⲁⲣⲉϥⲁⲣⲛⲁ ⲙ̅ⲡⲕⲟⲥⲙⲟⲥ
ⲡⲉϫⲉⲓ̅ⲥ̅ ϫⲉ ⲙ̅ⲡⲏⲩⲉⲛⲁⲃⲱⲗ̣ ⲟⲩⲧⲉ ⲕⲁϩ̣
ⲙ̅ⲡⲉⲧⲛ̅ⲙ̅ⲧ̅ⲟ ⲉⲃⲟⲗⲁⲩⲱ ⲡⲉⲧ̣ⲟⲛ̅ϩ ⲉⲃⲟⲗ ϩⲛ̅
ⲡⲉⲧⲟⲛ̅ϩ ⲛ̅ⲛⲁⲛⲁⲩ ⲁⲛ ⲉⲙⲟⲩ ⲟⲩ ϫⲟⲧ ⲓ̅ⲥ̅
ϫⲱ ⲙ̅ⲙⲟⲥ ϫⲉⲡⲉⲧⲁϩⲉⲣⲟⲩ ⲟⲩ̣ⲁ̣ⲁ̣ϥ ⲡ̣ⲕⲟⲥ
ⲙⲟⲥ ⲙ̅ⲡ̅ϣⲁ ⲙ̅ⲙⲟϥ ⲁⲛ ⲡⲉϫⲉ ⲓ̅ⲥ̅ ⲟ̣ⲩⲟ̣ⲓ̈
ⲛ̅ⲧⲥⲁⲣⲝ ⲧⲁⲉⲓ ⲉⲧⲟ̅ϣⲉ ⲛ̅ⲧ̅ ⲯⲩⲭⲏ ⲟ̣ⲩⲟⲓ̈
ⲛ̅ⲧ̅ ⲯⲩⲭⲏ ⲧⲁⲉⲓ ⲉⲧⲟ̅ϣ ⲉ ⲛ̅ⲧ̅ⲥⲁⲣⲝ ⲡⲉϫⲉ ⲓ̅ⲥ̅
ⲛⲁϥ ⲛ̅ϭⲓⲛⲉϥⲙⲁⲑⲏⲧⲏⲥ ϫⲉ ⲁϣ ⲛ̅ϩⲟⲟ
ⲉⲥⲛⲛⲏ ⲩ ⲛⲁⲛ ⲁⲩⲱ ⲟⲟⲩ ⲉⲥⲛⲛ̅ⲏⲩ ⲁⲛ ⲧ̅ⲟⲟ̣
ⲟ̅ⲩ̣ ⲙ̣ⲡⲉⲧ̅ⲉⲣⲟ ⲙⲉⲩⲛⲁ ⲭⲟⲟⲥ ϫⲉ ⲉⲓⲥ ϩⲏ
ⲧⲉ ⲙⲡⲓⲥⲁ ⲙⲉⲕⲉⲓ̈ⲥⲁ ⲏⲛ̅ⲧⲉ ⲧⲙ̅ⲛ̅ⲧⲣ ⲟ
ⲙⲡⲉⲓ̅ⲱⲧ̅ ⲉⲥⲡⲟⲣ̅ϣ ⲉⲃⲟⲗ ϩⲓ̈ϫⲙ̅ ⲡⲕ̅ⲁϩ ⲁⲩⲱ
ⲣⲣⲱⲙⲉ ⲛⲁⲩ ⲁ̣ⲛ̅ ⲉⲣⲟⲥ ⲡⲉϫⲉⲥⲓⲙⲱⲛ ⲡⲉⲧ̅ⲣⲟ
ⲛ̅ⲁⲩ ϫⲉ ⲙⲁⲣⲉ ⲙⲁⲣⲓ̈ϩⲁⲙ ⲉⲓ̅ ⲉⲃⲟⲗ ⲛ̅ϩⲏⲧ̅ⲛ̅
ϫⲉ ⲛⲉⲥϩⲓⲟⲙⲉ ⲙ̅ⲡ̅ϣⲁ ⲁⲛ ⲙ̅ⲡⲱⲛϩ̅ ⲡⲉϫⲉ ⲓ̅ⲥ̅
ϫⲉ ⲉⲓⲥ ϩⲏⲏⲧⲉ ⲁⲛⲟⲕ̅ ϯⲛⲁⲥ̅ⲱ̅ⲕ̅ ⲙ̅ⲙⲟⲥ
ϫⲉⲕⲁⲁⲥ ⲉⲛⲁⲁⲥ ⲛ̅ϩⲟⲟⲩⲧ̅ ϣⲓⲛⲁ ⲉⲥⲛⲁ ϣⲱ̣
ⲡⲉ ϩⲱⲱⲥ ⲉ ⲛⲟⲩ ⲡ̅ⲛ̅ⲁ̅ ⲉϥⲟⲛ ϩ̅ ⲉϥ ⲉⲓⲛⲉ ⲙ̅
ⲙⲱⲧⲛ̅ ⲛ̅ϩⲟⲟⲩⲧ̅ ϫⲉ ⲥϩⲓ̈ⲙⲉ ⲛⲓⲙ ⲉⲥⲛ̅ⲁⲉ̣
ⲛ̅ⲧ̅ⲟⲟⲩⲧ̅ ⲥⲛⲁⲃⲱⲕ̅ ⲉϩ̅ⲟⲩ̅ⲛ̅ ⲉⲧⲙ̅ⲛ̅ⲧⲉⲣ
ⲟ ⲛ̅ⲙ̅ⲡⲏⲩⲉ ⁘⁘⁘⁘⁘⁘⁘⁘⁘⁘⁘⁘⁘⁘⁘⁘⁘⁘

ⲡⲉⲩⲁⲅⲅⲉⲗⲓⲟⲛ

ⲡ̅ⲕⲁⲧⲁ ⲑⲱⲙⲁⲥ

ⲟⲩⲧⲉⲕⲣⲁ̣ⲓ̣ⲟⲥ ⲣ̅ⲣⲱⲙⲉ ⲛ̅ⲧⲁⲙⲓⲉ ϩⲉⲃⲣⲁ
ⲟⲥ ⲁⲩⲱ ϣⲁⲩⲙⲟⲩⲧⲉ ⲟⲩ ⲛ̅ⲧⲉ ⲩ̅ⲙⲓⲛ̅ⲉ
ϫⲉ ⲡ̅ⲣⲟ ⲥ̅ⲏⲗⲩⲧⲟⲥ ⲟⲩ ⲓⲟⲥ ⲇⲉ ⲁ̣ⲛ̣
ⲧⲁⲙⲓⲉ ⲡ̅ⲣⲟ ⲥ̅ⲏⲗⲩⲧ̣
ⲥⲉ ⲙ̅ⲟⲟⲡ ⲛ̅ⲑⲉ ⲉ ⲧ̅ⲟⲩ
ⲁⲩⲱ ⲥⲉ ⲧⲁⲙⲉⲓⲟ ⲛ̅ⲛ̅ⲕⲟⲟⲩ̣

THE GOSPEL OF THOMAS

The Hidden Sayings of Jesus

TRANSLATION, WITH INTRODUCTION, CRITICAL
EDITION OF THE COPTIC TEXT & NOTES BY
MARVIN MEYER

With an interpretation by
HAROLD BLOOM

HarperSanFrancisco
A Division of HarperCollins*Publishers*

FIRST EDITION

Library of Congress Cataloging-in-Publication Data

Gospel of Thomas. English.
  The Gospel of Thomas : the hidden sayings of Jesus / translation, with introduction, critical edition of the Coptic text, & notes by Marvin Meyer ; with an interpretation by Harold Bloom.—1st ed.
      p.   cm.
  Includes bibliographical references.
  ISBN 0-06-065581-X (alk. paper)
  1. Gospel of Thomas—Criticism, interpretation, etc.
  I. Meyer, Marvin. II. Bloom, Harold. III. Title.
  BS2860.T5A3   1992   91-58913
  229'.8—dc20   CIP

00 01 02 HAD 17 16

This edition is printed on recycled, acid-free paper that meets the American National Standards Institute z39.48 Standard.
Harper San Francisco and the author, in association with the Rainforest Action Network, will facilitate the planting of two trees for every one tree used in the manufacture of this book.

To Elisabeth

Contents

ACKNOWLEDGMENTS

I wish to express my appreciation to several people and organizations who have helped make this book a reality. I thank Gawdat Gabra, Girgis Daoud Girgis, and Samiha Abd El Shaheed of the Coptic Museum for their kindness in allowing me access to the Coptic pages of the Gospel of Thomas. I acknowledge the generous support of the National Endowment for the Humanities, the Graves Awards Committee (for the American Council of Learned Societies), and the Griset Chair in Religion at Chapman University. I appreciate very much the provocative and literate essay contributed by Harold Bloom, the eminent literary critic and student of ancient and modern *gnōsis*. I am grateful to Jonathan Reed of the University of La Verne for computer assistance in preparing the Coptic text for press. I also would like to thank a number of people at Chapman University and Harper San Francisco for their help in moving this project along, especially my editor, John Loudon, who invited me to put together this volume and worked closely with me to assure an uncompromising blend of scholarship and accessibility. Finally, I owe much to the continuing patience and support of my wife and children. It is to my daughter, who already has taught me a great deal about wisdom, that I dedicate this book.

Marvin W. Meyer
Chapman University

пєтаде єөєрмниєіа ⲚⲚⲉⲉⲓϣⲁⲭⲉ
ϥⲛⲁϫⲓ ϯⲡⲉ ⲁⲛ Ⲙⲡⲙⲟⲩ

GOSPEL OF THOMAS SAYING I

Introduction

The Gospel according to Thomas is an ancient collection of sayings of Jesus said to have been recorded by Judas Thomas the Twin. Unlike other early Christian gospels, which typically consist of narrative accounts interpreting the life of Jesus of Nazareth and culminating in descriptions of his death, the Gospel of Thomas focuses specifically upon sayings of Jesus. The document claims that these sayings themselves, when properly understood, communicate salvation and life: "Whoever discovers the interpretation of these sayings will not taste death" (saying 1).

The Coptic text of the Gospel of Thomas came to light with the discovery of the Nag Hammadi library, within which the Gospel of Thomas is to be found as the second tractate, or document, of Codex II. According to Muhammad Ali of the al-Samman clan, who has told his story to James M. Robinson, this remarkable manuscript discovery took place around December 1945.

At that time (so the story goes), several Egyptian fellahin, including Muhammad Ali, were riding their camels near the Jabal al-Tarif, a huge cliff that flanks the Nile River in Upper Egypt not far from the modern city of Nag Hammadi. They were looking for sabakh, a natural fertilizer that accumulates in the area, and so they hobbled their camels at the foot of the Jabal al-Tarif and began to dig around a large boulder that had fallen onto the talus, or slope of debris against the cliff face. Much to their surprise, they uncovered a large storage jar with a bowl sealed on top of it as a lid. Muhammad Ali hesitated before opening the sealed jar. Apparently he feared that the jar could contain a jinn, or spirit, that might be released to haunt him and do mischief. Yet he also reflected upon the legends concerning treasures hidden in the area, and his love of gold overcame his fear of jinns. He smashed the jar with his mattock, and as he has explained it, a golden substance flew out of the jar and disappeared into the air.

As we "demythologize" his story, we conclude that what he saw was probably neither a jinn nor gold, but rather papyrus fragments that were golden in color and that glistened in the sunlight. For he had discovered the thirteen papyrus books ("codices") of the Nag Hammadi library, and the Gospel of Thomas within the library.

Prior to this manuscript discovery, scholars knew of scattered statements in the church fathers referring to a document called the Gospel of Thomas. We suspect that some of these testimonies may well refer to the Infancy Gospel of Thomas, an early Christian document that presents a series of legendary tales about the miraculous feats of the child Jesus. Other testimonies suggest that a Gospel of Thomas was used or even written by the Manichaeans, who were mystical, gnostic followers of the teacher Mani. In his Catechesis 6.31, Cyril of Jerusalem claims that the Thomas who wrote the Gospel of Thomas was not one of the followers of Jesus but instead a wicked follower of Mani. The fairly extensive parallels between the Gospel of Thomas from the Nag Hammadi library and Manichaean literature may substantiate that there was a connection between the Nag Hammadi Gospel and a gospel in use among the Manichaeans.

Other testimonies in the church fathers refer more obviously to elements in the Gospel of Thomas from the Nag Hammadi library. The most secure of these references occurs in the third-century author Hippolytus of Rome. In his Refutation of All Heresies 5.7.20–21, he cites a statement from a Gospel of Thomas that was in use among the Naassene gnostics and that bears considerable similarity to part of Gospel of Thomas saying 4. The passage in Hippolytus reads as follows:

> <And> not only the mysteries of the Assyrians and the Phrygians <but also those of the Egyptians>, they say, bear witness to their doctrine about the blessed nature, both hidden and revealed, of what has been and is and is yet to be, which, he says, is <the> kingdom of heaven within humankind that is sought, concerning which they explicitly teach in the Gospel entitled

According to Thomas, saying thus, "One who seeks will find me in children from seven years, for there, hidden in the fourteenth age, I am revealed." And this comes not from Christ but from Hippocrates, saying, "A child of seven years is half a father." Hence, having placed the generative nature of all in the generative seed, and having heard the Hippocratic (saying) that a child of seven years is half a father, they say that one is revealed at four<teen> years according to Thomas. This is the unutterable and mystical doctrine they have.

Later, in Refutation 5.8.32, Hippolytus quotes another Naassene statement that is not explicitly said to derive from the Gospel of Thomas, but resembles a portion of Thomas saying 11: "So they say, 'If you ate dead things and made them living, what will you do if you eat living things?'"

In addition to these testimonies in the church fathers, three Greek papyri found in a rubbish heap at Oxyrhynchus (modern Bahnasa, Egypt) and published in 1897 and 1904 may also be linked to the Gospel of Thomas. These three papyri, Papyrus Oxyrhynchus 1, 654, and 655, all contain sayings of Jesus. Papyrus Oxyrhynchus 654.1–3 provides an incipit, or opening of the text, that is nearly identical to the prologue of the Nag Hammadi Gospel of Thomas: "These are the [hidden] sayings [that] the living Jesus spoke [and Judas, who is] also (called) Thomas, [recorded]." Other sayings contained in these three papyri parallel Gospel of Thomas sayings 1–7, 24, 26–33, 36–39, and 77. When he published *The Sayings of Jesus from Oxyrhynchus* in 1920, Hugh G. Evelyn-White conjectured that these sayings in the Oxyrhynchus papyri may come from the Gospel of Thomas, the Gospel of the Egyptians, or the Gospel of the Hebrews. Now that we know of the Gospel of Thomas from the Nag Hammadi library, we can appreciate how insightful Evelyn-White's observations were: The Oxyrhynchus papyri represent Greek editions of the Gospel of Thomas.

As a collection of sayings of Jesus, the Gospel of Thomas is closer in genre to other ancient collections of sayings than to the New

Testament gospels. In the ancient world, Jewish, Greco-Roman, and Christian collections of sayings circulated widely. Sayings are particularly prominent in Jewish wisdom literature. Jewish sages compiled documents like Proverbs, Ecclesiastes, the Wisdom of Solomon, and Sirach, as well as the tractate Pirke Aboth ("Sayings of the Fathers"), which was included within the Mishnah. These documents belong to an exceedingly old tradition of wisdom literature in Egypt and the ancient Middle East, a tradition that extends back to the second and third millennia B.C.E. with such collections as those of Amenemhat, Amenemope, Ptahhotep, Shuruppak, and Ahikar. The Jewish wisdom texts commonly personify Wisdom as a female character (the Hebrew and Greek words for wisdom, *hokhmah* and *sophia,* are both feminine) who comes from God and speaks forth in proverbs, riddles, and other sagacious sayings (see Proverbs 8:1–36).

Greco-Roman rhetoricians, especially those with a Cynic proclivity to use clever and incisive sayings, employed memorable statements called *chreiai* ("useful sayings") in their pedagogical exercises. *Chreiai* also were wise sayings, and the determining characteristic of *chreiai,* according to Greco-Roman rhetoricians, was that they were attributed appropriately to specific speakers. Often these sayings reflect a Cynic wit and a Cynic "bite." For instance: "Marcus Porcius Cato, when asked why he was studying Greek literature after his eightieth year, said, 'Not that I may die learned but that I may not die unlearned.'" And: "The Pythagorean philosopher Theano, when asked by someone how long it takes after having sex with a man for a woman to be pure to go to the Thesmophoria, said, 'If it is with her own husband, at once, but if with someone else's, never.'" *Chreiai* continued to be used by scholars of grammar and rhetoric into the Middle Ages, but among these medieval Christian rhetoricians the *chreiai* seem to have lost their Cynic spark. They became more domesticated exercises meant to serve the serious purposes of Christian theology and ethics.

The most well-known Christian collection of sayings is what Burton Mack calls "the lost gospel" Q (from the German *Quelle,* "source"), which was used, along with Mark, by Matthew and Luke in the compilation of their gospels. As it has been reconstructed out of sayings in Matthew and Luke, Q was very likely a "gospel" of wisdom very much like the Gospel of Thomas in its literary genre, its orientation toward wisdom, and even some of its actual contents. Like Thomas—and like *chreiai*—Q ordinarily attributed the wise sayings to a particular speaker, namely Jesus in these early Christian works. Once, however, Wisdom herself speaks forth in Q to announce that she will send forth prophets and apostles (see Luke 11:49; in Matthew 23:34 the words of Wisdom are put on the lips of Jesus). Elsewhere in Q Jesus and John are said to be the children of Wisdom (Luke 7:35; in Matthew 11:19 the reference is to the works of Wisdom). Luke 13:34–35 and Matthew 23:37–39 employ the vivid image of a hen and her chicks to attribute to Jesus a saying reminiscent of Wisdom, and Luke 10:21–22 and Matthew 11:25–27 likewise use motifs typical of Wisdom to have Jesus discuss how the father and the son are to be known. These sayings in Q illustrate how closely Jesus and Wisdom may be associated in a Christian sayings collection.

In preserving wise sayings attributed to Jesus, the Gospel of Thomas thus belongs to a rich heritage of sayings collections. The text of the Nag Hammadi Gospel of Thomas is preserved in Coptic, the late form of the Egyptian language in use from the Roman period on. Presumably the Gospel was originally composed in Greek, though a minority of scholars propose Syriac or Aramaic as the language of composition. The differences among the three Greek fragments from Oxyrhynchus and the Coptic text indicate that there were several editions of the Gospel of Thomas in circulation, and that modifications could be worked into these editions with some ease.

The 114 sayings in Thomas, as they are conventionally numbered, are presented in what appears to be more or less random order. At times, however, the sequence of sayings may be due to catchword connections (for example, sayings 25–26 both use the Coptic words for "brother" and "eye"); thematic interests (for example, sayings 12–13 stress the authority of James the Just and the preeminent authority of Thomas); formal similarities (for example, sayings 8–9, 63–65, and 96–98 are parables); or a possible reliance upon an oral or written source (for example, sayings 32–33, 43–45, 65–66, and 92–94 employ an arrangement of sayings similar to that in the New Testament synoptic gospels).

Since the earliest of the Greek Oxyrhynchus fragments has been assigned a date of around 200 C.E., the Gospel of Thomas must have been composed during the second century or even the latter part of the first century C.E. Considering the prominent place of Thomas in Syrian Christianity, we may suppose that the Gospel of Thomas was composed in Syria, possibly at Edessa (modern Urfa), where the memory of Thomas was revered and where, it is said, even his bones were venerated.

Today the papyrus pages of the Gospel of Thomas are housed at several museums and libraries around the world. The Coptic Gospel of Thomas is conserved at the Coptic Museum in Old Cairo, Egypt, and Papyrus Oxyrhynchus 1, 654, and 655 are to be found, respectively, in the Bodleian Library at Oxford University, the British Library in London, and Houghton Library at Harvard University.

———

As a gospel of wisdom, the Gospel of Thomas proclaims a distinctive message. In contrast to the way in which he is portrayed in other gospels, particularly New Testament gospels, Jesus in the Gospel of Thomas performs no physical miracles, reveals no fulfillment of prophecy, announces no apocalyptic kingdom about to disrupt the world order, and dies for no one's sins. Instead, Thomas's Jesus dispenses insight from the bubbling spring of wisdom (saying 13), discounts the value of prophecy and its fulfillment (saying 52), critiques end-of-the-world, apocalyptic announcements (sayings 51, 113), and offers a way of salvation through an encounter with the sayings of "the living Jesus."

The readers of the Gospel of Thomas are invited to join the quest for meaning in life by interpreting the oftentimes cryptic and enigmatic "hidden sayings" of Jesus. Saying 2 describes the vicissitudes of such a quest for insight: "Jesus said, 'Let one who seeks not stop seeking until one finds. When one finds, one will be troubled. When one is troubled, one will marvel and will rule over all'" (Papyrus Oxyrhynchus 654.8–9 adds, "and [having ruled], one will [rest]"). That is to say, the quest for meaning is to be undertaken with commitment; and while the way taken may be upsetting, people will attain insight and rest if only they persevere. For it is in the quest and through the quest that people find themselves and God. Then, according to the Gospel of Thomas, they discover that God's kingdom is not only outside them, but also inside them, that they are "children of the living father" (saying 3), and that they are essentially one with the savior. Saying 108 makes this point by using mystical language: "Jesus said, 'Whoever drinks from my mouth will become like me; I myself shall become that person, and the hidden things will be revealed to that person.'"

The hidden wisdom of Jesus in the Gospel of Thomas takes several forms. Some of Jesus' sayings in Thomas disclose an everyday sort of wisdom about life in the world that is familiar from other wisdom documents in the Jewish scriptures and elsewhere. Saying 21, for instance, recommends vigilance against the attacks of thieves. Saying 25 enjoins love for one's companion. Saying 26 advises that honest self-examination should precede the scrutiny and criticism of another, and saying 31 recognizes that familiarity breeds contempt.

Other sayings in Thomas suggest a more provocative and radical kind of wisdom that subverts the conventions of polite society. In *Q-Thomas Reader,* Stephen Patterson aptly calls this "counter-culture wisdom" (p. 94). Thus saying 55 has Jesus declare that true discipleship entails rejection of father, mother, brothers, and sisters. Saying 42, in which Jesus says, "Be passersby," seems to oppose a settled, comfortable lifestyle in favor of an unattached existence, perhaps like that of a wandering, homeless teacher. In saying 14 Jesus scoffs at the polite amenities of religious piety (fasting, praying, giving to charity). The conclusion to the parable in saying 64 excludes businesspeople from God's kingdom; saying 78 ridicules the luxurious life of the powerful. In saying 95 Jesus counsels lenders to give money away; while in saying 110 he encourages people of wealth and stature to "renounce the world." The parable in saying 98 even compares God's kingdom to the work of an assassin!

A few other sayings in the Gospel of Thomas show a more esoteric interest in transcending the world and identifying with the divine. Sometimes scholars have considered such sayings to be representative of a gnostic point of view, and they have classified the Gospel of Thomas, in its present form, as a gnostic document. (Ancient gnostics were religious people who sought true knowledge [in Greek, *gnōsis*] in a wide variety of traditions. They regarded attainment of knowledge as the key to a salvation that emphasized the mystical awakening of the self, the god within. Many gnostics were dualists in that they contrasted the divine world of light above with the fallen, created world of darkness below.) Among these more mystical and gnosticizing sayings in Thomas is saying 50, in which Jesus explains that when his followers dialogue with "them" (probably the powers of the world), they are to assert that their origin is in the divine light, that they are children of the light, and that the evidence of the indwelling of the divine is "motion and rest." Several features of this saying (answers to the powers, origin in the light, motion and rest) are typical of gnostic passages in other documents, for example the Secret Book ("Apocryphon") of John. Yet ancient gnosticism remains an elusive and highly syncretistic phenomenon, and scholars continue to debate how gnosticism should be defined and how gnostic groups should be identified. As a result it is difficult to call the Gospel of Thomas a gnostic gospel without considerable qualification, and we do well to exercise caution in classifying the text.

Although the Gospel of Thomas as a whole shows the particular characteristics of a collection of wisdom sayings and differs substantially from the narrative gospels of the New Testament, the individual sayings in Thomas commonly parallel sayings of Jesus in the synoptic gospels (and Q). Some of these parallels are very close. For instance, saying 54 has Jesus utter a familiar beatitude: "Fortunate are the poor, for yours is heaven's kingdom." This may be compared with the saying from Q that is now found in the Gospels of Matthew and Luke. Matthew 5:3 reads, "Fortunate are the poor in spirit, for theirs is heaven's kingdom," and Luke 6:20 reads, "Fortunate are you poor, for yours is God's kingdom." Saying 54 of the Gospel of Thomas obviously is very similar to each of the New Testament versions of this beatitude, and the saying in Thomas shares some features with Matthew and some with Luke. Completely absent, though, is Matthew's spiritualization of the beatitude.

Parallels like these make it clear that there must be a direct or indirect relationship among the Gospel of Thomas, Q, and the synoptic gospels, but scholars have not been able to agree on what that relationship might be. Three basic explanations have been offered. Some scholars have suggested that the Gospel of Thomas is dependent upon the synoptic gospels and so is a secondary collection of sayings drawn from the New Testament. Other scholars have posited that the Gospel of Thomas is independent of the New Testament synoptic gospels, but is related to oral or written traditions similar to those behind the synoptic gospels (compare Q). Still others have observed that the process of composing the Gospel of Thomas may have been more complex than either of the first two explanations would suggest. As Ron Cameron writes in his article on the Gospel of Thomas in *The Anchor Bible Dictionary,* "An intertextual model may prove helpful, for it enables texts to be understood as highly conscious authorial compositions, adapted and adopted from various encounters with groups and repeated engagements with texts that constituted the cultural tapestry of the times" (p. 537).

However this may be, an excellent case can be made for the position that the Gospel of Thomas is not fundamentally dependent upon the New Testament gospels, but that it preserves sayings that at times appear to be more original than the New Testament parallels. An illustration of this point may be Gospel of Thomas saying 9:

> Jesus said, "Look, the sower went out, took a handful (of seeds), and scattered (them). Some fell on the road, and the birds

came and pecked them up. Others fell on rock, and they did not take root in the soil and did not produce heads of grain. Others fell on thorns, and they choked the seeds and worms devoured them. And others fell on good soil, and it brought forth a good crop: It yielded sixty per measure and one hundred twenty per measure."

This saying, known as the parable of the sower, is also preserved in all three synoptic gospels: Matthew 13:3–9, Mark 4:2–9, Luke 8:4–8. In each instance in the New Testament gospels, the parable itself is followed by an allegorical interpretation (see Matthew 13:18–23, Mark 4:13–20, Luke 8:11–15) that applies the elements of the parable to the life of the church. It is widely acknowledged among scholars that these allegorical interpretations were produced by the early church as Christians attempted to apply the details of a parable about farming in rural Palestine to features of church life during the latter half of the first century.

The absence of allegorical interpretations in connection with this and other parables in the Gospel of Thomas helps confirm that such elements were added later. In the instance of the parable of the sower, the Gospel of Thomas thus presents the parable in a more original form than any of the New Testament gospels. Further, the parable in Thomas retains at least one item that is not found in the New Testament versions and that may constitute a very early storyteller's detail: the sower "took a handful (of seeds)."

The value of the Gospel of Thomas as a primary source for the Jesus tradition is underscored by the presence within Thomas of sayings of Jesus not included in the New Testament and sometimes totally unknown prior to the discovery of this gospel. Saying 97, the parable of the jar of meal, describes the fragile, elusive quality of God's kingdom:

Jesus said, "The [father's] kingdom is like a woman who was carrying a [jar] full of meal. While she was walking along [a] distant road, the handle of the jar broke and the meal spilled behind her [along] the road. She did not know it; she had not noticed a problem. When she reached her house, she put the jar down and discovered that it was empty."

Saying 98, the previously mentioned parable of the assassin, employs the violent images of first-century Palestine to proclaim the need for readiness and vigor in the face of God's kingdom:

> Jesus said, "The father's kingdom is like a person who wanted to put someone powerful to death. While at home he drew his sword and thrust it into the wall to find out whether his hand would go in. Then he killed the powerful one."

At its recent meetings the Jesus Seminar, a scholarly group founded by Robert Funk for the purpose of examining the Jesus tradition, voted that both of these hitherto unknown parables merit serious consideration as sayings that may go back, in something like this form, to the historical person of Jesus.

What, then, do all these sayings in the Gospel of Thomas contribute to our knowledge of Jesus of Nazareth? In order to answer this question, we first note that during the twentieth century the dominant paradigm for understanding the historical Jesus has been that of Jesus the apocalyptic or eschatological figure who announced the imminent breaking in of God's kingdom. In his book *The Quest of the Historical Jesus,* Albert Schweitzer vividly portrayed the eschatological focus of the career of Jesus:

> There is silence all around. The Baptist appears, and cries: "Repent, for the Kingdom of Heaven is at hand." Soon after that comes Jesus, and in the knowledge that he is the coming Son of Man lays hold of the wheel of the world to set it moving on that last revolution which is to bring all ordinary history to a close. It refuses to turn, and he throws himself upon it. Then it does turn; and crushes him. Instead of bringing in the eschatological conditions, he has destroyed them. The wheel rolls onward, and the mangled body of the one immeasurably great Man, who was strong enough to think of himself as the spiritual ruler of

mankind and to bend history to his purpose, is hanging upon it still. That is his victory and his reign. (pp. 370–71)

While many scholars have disagreed with aspects of this portrayal, Schweitzer's emphasis upon the eschatological dimension of Jesus' ministry has dominated the modern quest for the Jesus of history.

Now, thanks to serious scholarship on the Gospel of Thomas and Q, another paradigm for interpreting Jesus is emerging. This paradigm suggests that especially in Jesus' sayings of wisdom, we may glimpse something of the historical Jesus. According to this way of understanding Jesus, he may not have been an apocalyptic figure at all. In the Gospel of Thomas and the first version of Q, Jesus does not use apocalyptic images to announce the coming of God's kingdom, but rather declares that the kingdom is already a present reality. Saying 113 makes this point clear:

> His followers said to him, "When will the kingdom come?"
> "It will not come by watching for it. It will not be said, 'Look, here it is,' or 'Look, there it is.' Rather, the father's kingdom is spread out upon the earth, and people do not see it."

Saying 3 uses somewhat similar language to state that "the kingdom is inside you and it is outside you." As a teacher with a non-apocalyptic message, Jesus according to this paradigm wandered (or passed by; compare saying 42) through the towns and the countryside of Galilee. While wandering from place to place, he uttered parables and clever sayings—sayings of wisdom—in order to make those around him confront a new and compelling vision of life.

In these respects the person of Jesus, so understood, may begin to resemble that of an itinerant Cynic teacher. Burton Mack puts it succinctly in his book *A Myth of Innocence:* "Jesus' wisdom incorporated the pungent invitation to insight and the daring to be different that characterized the Cynic approach to life" (p. 69). In *The Historical Jesus,* John Dominic Crossan expands upon this basic assessment of Jesus:

> The historical Jesus was, then, a *peasant Jewish Cynic.* His peasant village was close enough to a Greco-Roman city like

Sepphoris that sight and knowledge of Cynicism are neither inexplicable nor unlikely. But his work was among the farms and villages of Lower Galilee. His strategy, implicitly for himself and explicitly for his followers, was the combination of *free healing and common eating,* a religious and economic egalitarianism that negated alike and at once the hierarchical and patronal normalcies of Jewish religion and Roman power. . . . Miracle and parable, healing and eating were calculated to force individuals into unmediated physical and spiritual contact with God and unmediated physical and spiritual contact with one another. He announced, in other words, the brokerless kingdom of God. (pp. 421–22)

The Cynics emerged from the philosophical tradition of Socrates as social critics and popular philosophers who lived a simple life and employed sharp, witty sayings in order to make people raise questions about their own lives. The influence of the Cynics and other hellenistic thinkers is evident in the Galilee of the first century; Jewish wisdom literature itself bears the marks of hellenistic concerns. While in general the rhetoric of kingdom language functioned within Judaism to depict the rule of God or of political figures, the term "God's kingdom" never actually occurs in the Hebrew scriptures, though it does occur in Wisdom of Solomon 10:10. The word "kingdom" is also used, beyond Judaism, by the ancient author Epictetus to describe the Cynic life. Hence the kingdom emphasis of Jesus the Jewish teacher may be at home in a setting in which Jewish and Cynic interests coalesce, and his wisdom as preached in the Gospel of Thomas, with its persistent call to the quest for insight, may approach the wisdom of the Cynics.

———

The main purpose of this book is to present a fresh English translation of the Gospel of Thomas and a critically established Coptic text. The Coptic text is based upon previous work on the text and upon my own study of the document, under ultraviolet light, at the Coptic Museum during the summer of 1988. This new edition of the

Coptic text corrects inaccuracies and peculiarities of earlier editions while keeping textual emendations to a minimum. (Unlike other editors I have been especially chary of introducing a quotation formula—for example, "Jesus said"—where the text itself includes none.) In this book I use the following signs:

[   ]   Square brackets indicate a lacuna or gap in the text.

<   >   Pointed brackets indicate a correction of a scribal omission or error.

{   }   Braces indicate superfluous letters that presumably were added by a scribe.

(·)   Parentheses indicate material that is not present in the text but is supplied by the translator for the sake of clarity of translation.

Dots placed under Coptic letters indicate letters that are visually uncertain, and dots placed by themselves indicate ink traces that cannot be deciphered. Dots placed within square brackets in the Coptic text indicate the approximate number of letters missing in the text. In the English translation, three dots indicate a word or words that cannot be restored with confidence.

Manuscript page numbers are given in bold numerals in the Coptic text. (The text occupies page 32, line 10, through page 51, line 28, of the manuscript.) Raised vertical strokes designate the lines in the manuscript; every fifth line is indicated by means of a raised number.

In this edition of the Coptic text I present, for the sake of simplicity, the text alone, without the apostrophes (the word or unit dividers) that are employed by the Coptic scribe.

The English translation of the Gospel of Thomas is meant to be as accurate and as graceful as possible, yet I have tried not to offer a translation that glosses over difficulties and ambiguities in the Coptic text. Ordinarily I use inclusive language in the English translation:

The general spirit of the document recommends it, and the character of the Coptic language, which employs the masculine to refer to what is indefinite or neutral (there is no neuter gender in Coptic), allows such translational choices. I have not used inclusive language, however, when it might compromise the accuracy of the translation. I have also allowed a certain amount of gender bias to remain in the translation as a reflection of the specific contents of the text and the nature of the Coptic language.

To the Coptic text and English translation is added a series of notes. The notes address important problems and issues in the document and suggest alternate readings and translations of passages. They also refer to the most significant parallels to sayings in the Gospel of Thomas. When the parallel passages are not readily available in the Jewish scriptures or the New Testament, I ordinarily include English translations of the passages. I give special attention to the important variant readings in the parallel Oxyrhynchus papyri. The brief bibliography indicates works that I have consulted and other basic books and articles for further reading.

I am particularly pleased that Harold Bloom has agreed to contribute what he describes as "a gnostic sermon that takes the Gospel of Thomas for its text." Bloom's commentary suggests an interpretation of Thomas, along gnostic lines, as a text that may continue to speak to people engaged in a contemporary quest for knowledge and insight. I heartily concur with Bloom that "the hidden sayings" of Jesus may be understood in a gnostic way. Whether the text itself should be classified as gnostic, however, is another question altogether, a question that relates to scholarly issues of definition and taxonomy. Often agreeing and at times disagreeing with my own interpretation, Bloom maintains that "this Jesus is looking for the face he had before the world was made." I only wish to underscore Bloom's final appeal: "If such is your quest, then the Gospel of Thomas calls out to you."

The Gospel of Thomas

ⲚⲀⲈⲒ ⲚⲈ ⲚϢⲀϪⲈ ⲈⲐⲎⲠ ⲈⲚⲦⲀ ⲓ̅ⲥ̅ ⲈⲦⲞⲚϩ ϪⲞⲞⲨ
ⲀⲨⲱ ⲀϤⲤϩⲀⲒⲤⲞⲨ ⲚϬⲒ ⲆⲒⲆⲨⲘⲞⲤ ⲒⲞⲨⲆⲀⲤ
ⲐⲰⲘⲀⲤ

1 ⲀⲨⲱ ⲠⲈϪⲀϤ ϪⲈ ⲠⲈⲦⲀϩⲈ ⲈⲐⲈⲢⲘⲎⲚⲈⲒⲀ
ⲚⲚⲈⲈⲒϢⲀϪⲈ ϤⲚⲀϪⲒ ϯⲠⲈ ⲀⲚ ⲘⲠⲘⲞⲨ

2 ⲠⲈϪⲈ ⲓ̅ⲥ̅ ⲘⲚⲦⲢⲈϤ¹⁵ⲖⲞ ⲚϬⲒ ⲠⲈⲦϢⲒⲚⲈ ⲈϤϢⲒⲚⲈ
ϢⲀⲚⲦⲈϤϬⲒⲚⲈ ⲀⲨⲱ ϩⲞⲦⲀⲚ ⲈϤϢⲀⲚϬⲒⲚⲈ
ϤⲚⲀϢⲦⲢⲦⲢ̅ ⲀⲨⲱ ⲈϤϢⲀⲚϢⲦⲞⲢⲦⲢ̅ ϤⲚⲀⲢ̅ ϢⲠⲎⲢⲈ
ⲀⲨⲱ ϤⲚⲀⲢ̅ Ⲣ̅ⲢⲞ ⲈϪⲘ̅ ⲠⲦⲎⲢϤ

3 ⲠⲈϪⲈ ⲓ̅ⲥ̅ ϪⲈ ⲈⲨϢⲀ²⁰ϪⲞⲞⲤ ⲚⲎⲦⲚ̅ ⲚϬⲒ ⲚⲈⲦⲤⲰⲔ
ϩⲎⲦ ⲦⲎⲨⲦⲚ̅ ϪⲈ ⲈⲒⲤϩⲎⲎⲦⲈ ⲈⲦⲘ̅ⲚⲦⲈⲢⲞ ϩⲚ̅ ⲦⲠⲈ
ⲈⲈⲒⲈ Ⲛ̅ϩⲀⲖⲎⲦ ⲚⲀⲢ̅ ϢⲞⲢⲠ ⲈⲢⲰⲦⲚ̅ Ⲛ̅ⲦⲈ ⲦⲠⲈ
ⲈⲨϢⲀⲚϪⲞⲞⲤ ⲚⲎⲦⲚ̅ ϪⲈ ⲤϩⲚ̅ ⲐⲀⲖⲀⲤⲤⲀ ⲈⲈⲒⲈ
Ⲛ̅ⲦⲂⲦ ⲚⲀⲢ̅ ϢⲞⲢⲠ ⲈⲢⲰⲦⲚ̅ ²⁵ⲀⲖⲖⲀ ⲦⲘⲚ̅ⲦⲈⲢⲞ
ⲤⲘ̅ⲠⲈⲦⲚ̅ϩⲞⲨⲚ ⲀⲨⲱ ⲤⲘ̅ⲠⲈⲦⲚ̅ⲂⲀⲖ

ϩⲞⲦⲀⲚ ⲈⲦⲈⲦⲚ̅ϢⲀⲚⲤⲞⲨⲰⲚ ⲦⲎⲨⲦⲚ̅ ⲦⲞⲦⲈ
ⲤⲈⲚⲀⲤⲞⲨⲰⲚ ³³ⲦⲎⲚⲈ ⲀⲨⲱ ⲦⲈⲦⲚⲀⲈⲒⲘⲈ ϪⲈ Ⲛ̅ⲦⲰⲦⲚ̅
ⲠⲈ Ⲛ̅ϢⲎⲢⲈ ⲘⲠⲈⲒⲰⲦ ⲈⲦⲞⲚϩ ⲈϢⲰⲠⲈ ⲆⲈ
ⲦⲈⲦⲚⲀⲤⲞⲨⲰⲚ ⲦⲎⲨⲦⲚ̅ ⲀⲚ ⲈⲈⲒⲈ ⲦⲈⲦⲚ̅ϢⲞⲞⲠ ϩⲚ̅
ⲞⲨⲘⲚ̅ⲦϩⲎⲔⲈ ⲀⲨⲱ Ⲛ̅ⲦⲰⲦⲚ̅ ⁵ⲠⲈ ⲦⲘⲚ̅ⲦϩⲎⲔⲈ

4 ⲠⲈϪⲈ ⲓ̅ⲥ̅ ϤⲚⲀϪⲚⲀⲨ ⲀⲚ ⲚϬⲒ ⲠⲢⲰⲘⲈ Ⲛ̅ϩⲖ̅ⲖⲞ
ϩⲚ̅ ⲚⲈϤϩⲞⲞⲨ ⲈϪⲚⲈ ⲞⲨⲔⲞⲨⲈⲒ Ⲛ̅ϢⲎⲢⲈ ϢⲎⲘ ⲈϤϩⲚ̅
ⲤⲀϢϤ̅ Ⲛ̅ϩⲞⲞⲨ ⲈⲦⲂⲈ ⲠⲦⲞⲠⲞⲤ ⲘⲠⲰⲚϩ ⲀⲨⲱ
ϤⲚⲀⲰⲚϩ ϪⲈ ⲞⲨⲚ̅ ϩⲀϩ Ⲛ̅ϢⲞⲢⲠ ⲚⲀⲢ̅ ϩⲀ¹⁰Ⲉ ⲀⲨⲱ
Ⲛ̅ⲤⲈϢⲰⲠⲈ ⲞⲨⲀ ⲞⲨⲰⲦ

5 ⲠⲈϪⲈ ⲓ̅ⲥ̅ ⲤⲞⲨⲰⲚ ⲠⲈⲦⲘⲠⲘⲦⲞ ⲘⲠⲈⲔϩⲞ ⲈⲂⲞⲖ
ⲀⲨⲱ ⲠⲈⲐⲎⲠ ⲈⲢⲞⲔ ϤⲚⲀϬⲰⲖⲠ ⲈⲂⲞⲖ ⲚⲀⲔ ⲘⲚ̅
ⲖⲀⲀⲨ ⲄⲀⲢ ⲈϤϩⲎⲠ ⲈϤⲚⲀⲞⲨⲰⲚϩ ⲈⲂⲞⲖ ⲀⲚ

These are the hidden sayings that the living Jesus spoke and Judas Thomas the Twin recorded.

1   And he said, "Whoever discovers the interpretation of these sayings will not taste death."

2   Jesus said, "Let one who seeks not stop seeking until one finds. When one finds, one will be troubled. When one is troubled, one will marvel and will rule over all."

3   Jesus said, "If your leaders say to you, 'Look, the kingdom is in heaven,' then the birds of heaven will precede you. If they say to you, 'It is in the sea,' then the fish will precede you. Rather, the kingdom is inside you and it is outside you.

"When you know yourselves, then you will be known, and you will understand that you are children of the living father. But if you do not know yourselves, then you dwell in poverty, and you are poverty."

4   Jesus said, "The person old in days will not hesitate to ask a little child seven days old about the place of life, and that person will live. For many of the first will be last and will become a single one."

5   Jesus said, "Know what is in front of your face, and what is hidden from you will be disclosed to you. For there is nothing hidden that will not be revealed."

6   ⲁⲩⲍⲛⲟⲩϥ ⲛϭⲓ ⲛⲉϥⲙⲁⲑⲏⲧⲏⲥ [15] ⲡⲉⲍⲁⲩ ⲛⲁϥ
ⲍⲉⲕⲟⲩⲱϣ ⲉⲧⲣⲛ̄ⲣ̄ⲛⲏⲥⲧⲉⲩⲉ ⲁⲩⲱ ⲉϣ ⲧⲉ ⲑⲉ
ⲉⲛⲁϣⲗⲏⲗ ⲉⲛⲁϯ ⲉⲗⲉⲏⲙⲟⲥⲩⲛⲏ ⲁⲩⲱ
ⲉⲛⲁⲣ̄ⲡⲁⲣⲁⲧⲏⲣⲉⲓ ⲉⲟⲩ ⲛϭⲓⲟⲩⲱⲙ

ⲡⲉⲍⲉ ⲓ̄ⲥ̄ ⲍⲉ ⲙ̄ⲡⲣ̄ⲍⲉ ϭⲟⲗ ⲁⲩⲱ ⲡⲉⲧⲉⲧⲙ̄ⲙⲟⲥⲧⲉ
ⲙ̄ⲙⲟϥ ⲙ̄ⲡⲣ̄ⲁⲁϥ ⲍⲉ [20] ⲥⲉϭⲟⲗⲡ ⲧⲏⲣⲟⲩ ⲉⲃⲟⲗ
ⲙ̄ⲡⲉⲙⲧⲟ ⲉⲃⲟⲗ ⲛ̄ⲧⲡⲉ ⲙⲛ̄ ⲗⲁⲁⲩ ⲅⲁⲣ ⲉϥϩⲏⲡ
ⲉϥⲛⲁⲟⲩⲱⲛϩ ⲉⲃⲟⲗ ⲁⲛ ⲁⲩⲱ ⲙⲛ̄ ⲗⲁⲁⲩ ⲉϥϩⲟⲃⲥ̄
ⲉⲩ̄ⲛⲁϭⲱ ⲟⲩⲉϣⲛ̄ ϭⲟⲗⲡϥ

7   ⲡⲉⲍⲉ ⲓ̄ⲥ̄ ⲟⲩⲙⲁⲕⲁⲣⲓⲟⲥ ⲡⲉ ⲡⲙⲟⲩⲉⲓ ⲡⲁⲉⲓ ⲉⲧⲉ
[25] ⲡⲣⲱⲙⲉ ⲛⲁⲟⲩⲟⲙϥ ⲁⲩⲱ ⲛ̄ⲧⲉⲡⲙⲟⲩⲉⲓ ϣⲱⲡⲉ
ⲣ̄ⲣⲱⲙⲉ ⲁⲩⲱ ϥⲃⲏⲧ ⲛϭⲓ ⲡⲣⲱⲙⲉ ⲡⲁⲉⲓ ⲉⲧⲉ
ⲡⲙⲟⲩⲉⲓ ⲛⲁⲟⲩⲟⲙϥ ⲁⲩⲱ ⲡⲙⲟⲩⲉⲓ ⲛⲁϣⲱⲡⲉ
ⲣ̄ⲣⲱⲙⲉ

8   ⲁⲩⲱ ⲡⲉⲍⲁϥ ⲍⲉ ⲉⲡⲣⲱⲙⲉ ⲧⲛ̄ⲧⲱⲛ ⲁⲩⲟⲩⲱϩⲉ [30]
ⲣ̄ⲣⲙⲛ̄ϩⲏⲧ ⲡⲁⲉⲓ ⲛ̄ⲧⲁϩⲛⲟⲩⲍⲉ ⲛ̄ⲧⲉϥⲁⲃⲱ
ⲉⲑⲁⲗⲁⲥⲥⲁ ⲁϥⲥⲱⲕ ⲙ̄ⲙⲟⲥ ⲉϩⲣⲁⲓ ϩⲛ̄ ⲑⲁⲗⲁⲥⲥⲁ
ⲉⲥⲙⲉϩ ⲛ̄ⲧⲃⲧ ⲛ̄ⲕⲟⲩⲉⲓ ⲛ̄ϩⲣⲁⲓ ⲛ̄ϩⲏⲧⲟⲩ ⲁϥϩⲉ
ⲁⲩⲛⲟϭ ⲛ̄ⲧⲃⲧ ⲉⲛⲁⲛⲟⲩϥ ⲛϭⲓ ⲡⲟⲩⲱϩⲉ ⲣ̄ⲣⲙⲛ̄ϩⲏⲧ
ⲁϥⲛⲟⲩ [35] ⲍⲉ ⲛ̄ⲛⲕⲟⲩⲉⲓ ⲧⲏⲣⲟⲩ ⲛ̄ⲧⲃⲧ ⲉⲃⲟⲗ
ⲉ[ⲡⲉ]34ⲥⲏⲧ ⲉⲑⲁⲗⲁⲥⲥⲁ ⲁϥⲥⲱⲧⲡ ⲙ̄ⲡⲛⲟϭ ⲛ̄ⲧⲃⲧ
ⲭⲱⲣⲓⲥ ϩⲓⲥⲉ ⲡⲉⲧⲉ ⲟⲩⲛ̄ ⲙⲁⲁⲍⲉ ⲙ̄ⲙⲟϥ ⲉⲥⲱⲧⲙ̄
ⲙⲁⲣⲉϥⲥⲱⲧⲙ̄

9   ⲡⲉⲍⲉ ⲓ̄ⲥ̄ ⲍⲉ ⲉⲓⲥϩⲏⲏⲧⲉ ⲁϥⲉⲓ ⲉⲃⲟⲗ ⲛϭⲓ
ⲡⲉⲧⲥⲓⲧⲉ ⲁϥⲙⲉϩ ⲧⲟⲟⲧϥ̄ [5] ⲁϥⲛⲟⲩⲍⲉ ⲁϩⲟⲉⲓⲛⲉ ⲙⲉⲛ
ϩⲉ ⲉⲍⲛ̄ ⲧⲉϩⲓⲏ ⲁⲩⲉⲓ ⲛϭⲓ ⲛ̄ϩⲁⲗⲁⲧⲉ ⲁⲩⲕⲁⲧϥⲟⲩ
ϩⲛ̄ⲕⲟⲟⲩⲉ ⲁⲩϩⲉ ⲉⲍⲛ̄ ⲧⲡⲉⲧⲣⲁ ⲁⲩⲱ ⲙ̄ⲡⲟⲩⲍⲉ
ⲛⲟⲩⲛⲉ ⲉⲡⲉⲥⲏⲧ ⲉⲡⲕⲁϩ ⲁⲩⲱ ⲙ̄ⲡⲟⲩⲧⲉⲩⲉ ϩⲙⲥ̄
ⲉϩⲣⲁⲓ ⲉⲧⲡⲉ ⲁⲩⲱ ϩⲛ̄ⲕⲟⲟⲩⲉ ⲁⲩϩⲉ ⲉⲍⲛ̄
ⲛ̄ϣⲟⲛ10ⲧⲉ ⲁⲩⲱϭⲧ ⲙ̄ⲡⲉϭⲣⲟϭ ⲁⲩⲱ ⲁⲡϥⲛ̄ⲧ
ⲟⲩⲟⲙⲟⲩ ⲁⲩⲱ ⲁϩⲛ̄ⲕⲟⲟⲩⲉ ϩⲉ ⲉⲍⲛ̄ ⲡⲕⲁϩ
ⲉⲧⲛⲁⲛⲟⲩϥ ⲁⲩⲱ ⲁϥϯ ⲕⲁⲣⲡⲟⲥ ⲉϩⲣⲁⲓ ⲉⲧⲡⲉ
ⲉⲛⲁⲛⲟⲩ ⲁϥⲉⲓ ⲛ̄ⲥⲉ ⲉⲥⲟⲧⲉ ⲁⲩⲱ ϣⲉⲍⲟⲩⲱⲧ
ⲉⲥⲟⲧⲉ

6   His followers asked him and said to him, "Do you want us to fast? How should we pray? Should we give to charity? What diet should we observe?"

    Jesus said, "Do not lie, and do not do what you hate, because all things are disclosed before heaven. For there is nothing hidden that will not be revealed, and there is nothing covered that will remain undisclosed."

7   Jesus said, "Fortunate is the lion that the human will eat, so that the lion becomes human. And foul is the human that the lion will eat, and the lion will become human."

8   And he said, "Humankind is like a wise fisherman who cast his net into the sea and drew it up from the sea full of little fish. Among them the wise fisherman discovered a fine large fish. He threw all the little fish back into the sea and with no difficulty chose the large fish. Whoever has ears to hear should hear."

9   Jesus said, "Look, the sower went out, took a handful (of seeds), and scattered (them). Some fell on the road, and the birds came and pecked them up. Others fell on rock, and they did not take root in the soil and did not produce heads of grain. Others fell on thorns, and they choked the seeds and worms devoured them. And others fell on good soil, and it brought forth a good crop: It yielded sixty per measure and one hundred twenty per measure."

10 ПЕϪЕ ⲓⲥ ϪЕ ⲀЕІⲚⲞⲨϪЕ ⲚⲞⲨⲔⲰϩⲦ ЕϪⲚ [15]
ПⲔⲞⲤⲘⲞⲤ ⲀⲨⲰ ЕІⲤϨⲎⲎⲦЕ ϮⲀⲢЕϨ ЕⲢⲞϤ '
ϢⲀⲚⲦЕϤϪЕⲢⲞ

11 ПЕϪЕ ⲓⲥ ϪЕ ⲦЕЕІⲠЕ ⲚⲀⲢⲠⲀ'ⲢⲀⲄЕ ⲀⲨⲰ
ⲦЕⲦⲚⲦⲠЕ ⲘⲘⲞⲤ ⲚⲀⲢⲠⲀⲢⲀⲄЕ '

ⲀⲨⲰ ⲚЕⲦⲘⲞⲞⲨⲦ ⲤЕⲞⲚϨ ⲀⲚ ⲀⲨⲰ ⲚЕⲦⲞⲚϨ '
ⲤЕⲚⲀⲘⲞⲨ ⲀⲚ

ⲚϨⲞⲞⲨ ⲚЕⲦЕⲦⲚⲞⲨⲰⲘ [20] ⲘⲠЕⲦⲘⲞⲞⲨⲦ
ⲚЕⲦЕⲦⲚЕІⲢЕ ⲘⲘⲞϤ ⲘⲠЕ'ⲦⲞⲚϨ ϨⲞⲦⲀⲚ
ЕⲦЕⲦⲚϢⲀⲚϢⲰⲠЕ ϨⲘ ⲠⲞⲨ'ⲞЕІⲚ ⲞⲨ ⲠЕⲦЕⲦⲚⲀⲀϤ

ϨⲘ ⲪⲞⲞⲨ ЕⲦЕⲦⲚ'Ⲟ ⲚⲞⲨⲀ ⲀⲦЕⲦⲚЕІⲢЕ ⲘⲠⲤⲚⲀⲨ
ϨⲞⲦⲀⲚ ϪЕ 'ЕⲦЕⲦⲚϢⲀϢⲰⲠЕ ⲚⲤⲚⲀⲨ ⲞⲨ ⲠЕ
ЕⲦЕ [25] ⲦⲚⲚⲀⲀϤ

12 ПЕϪЕ ⲘⲘⲀⲐⲎⲦⲎⲤ Ⲛⲓⲥ ϪЕ ⲦⲚ'ⲤⲞⲞⲨⲚ ϪЕ
ⲔⲚⲀⲂⲰⲔ ⲚⲦⲞⲞⲦⲚ ⲚІⲘ ⲠЕ'ЕⲦⲚⲀⲢ ⲚⲞϬ ЕϨⲢⲀⲒ
ЕϪⲰⲚ

ПЕϪЕ ⲓⲥ ⲚⲀⲨ'ϪЕ ⲠⲘⲀ ⲚⲦⲀⲦЕⲦⲚЕІ ⲘⲘⲀⲨ
ЕⲦЕⲦⲚⲀⲂⲰⲔ ϢⲀ ⲒⲀⲔⲰⲂⲞⲤ ⲠϪІⲔⲀІⲞⲤ ⲠⲀЕІ
ⲚⲦⲀ [30] ⲦⲠЕ ⲘⲚ ⲠⲔⲀϨ ϢⲰⲠЕ ЕⲦⲂⲎⲦϤ

10   Jesus said, "I have thrown fire upon the world, and look, I am watching it until it blazes."

11   Jesus said, "This heaven will pass away, and the one above it will pass away.

"The dead are not alive, and the living will not die.

"During the days when you ate what is dead, you made it alive. When you are in the light, what will you do?

"On the day when you were one, you became two. But when you become two, what will you do?"

12   The followers said to Jesus, "We know that you are going to leave us. Who will be our leader?"

Jesus said to them, "No matter where you are, you are to go to James the Just, for whose sake heaven and earth came into being."

13 ΠΕϪΕ ⲓ̅ⲥ̅ ' Ⲛ̅ⲚⲈϤⲘⲀⲐⲎⲦⲎⲤ ϪⲈ ⲦⲚ̅ⲦⲰⲚⲦ
Ⲛ̅ⲦⲈⲦⲚ̅ϪⲞⲞⲤ ⲚⲀⲈⲒ ϪⲈ ⲈⲈⲒⲚⲈ Ⲛ̅ⲚⲒⲘ

ΠⲈϪⲀϤ ⲚⲀϤ ' Ⲛ̅ϬⲒ ⲤⲒⲘⲰⲚ ⲠⲈⲦⲢⲞⲤ ϪⲈ ⲈⲔⲈⲒⲚⲈ
Ⲛ̅ⲞⲨⲀⲅ̔ⲅ̔ⲈⲖⲞⲤ Ⲛ̅ⲆⲒⲔⲀⲒⲞⲤ

ΠⲈϪⲀϤ ⲚⲀϤ Ⲛ̅ϬⲒ ⲘⲀⲐ35ⲐⲀⲒⲞⲤ ϪⲈ ⲈⲔⲈⲒⲚⲈ
Ⲛ̅ⲞⲨⲢⲰⲘⲈ Ⲙ̅ⲫⲒⲖⲞⲤⲞ̔ⲪⲞⲤ Ⲛ̅ⲢⲘ̅Ⲛ̅ϨⲎⲦ

ΠⲈϪⲀϤ ⲚⲀϤ Ⲛ̅ϬⲒ ⲐⲰⲘⲀⲤ ' ϪⲈ ⲠⲤⲀϨ ϨⲞⲖⲰⲤ
ⲦⲀⲦⲀⲠⲢⲞ ⲚⲀϢ«Ϣ›ⲀⲠϤ ⲀⲚ ' ⲈⲦⲢⲀϪⲞⲞⲤ ϪⲈ
ⲈⲔⲈⲒⲚⲈ Ⲛ̅ⲚⲒⲘ

ΠⲈϪⲈ ⲒⲎ̅ⲥ̅ [5] ϪⲈ ⲀⲚⲞⲔ ⲠⲈⲔⲤⲀϨ ⲀⲚ ⲈⲠⲈⲒ ⲀⲔⲤⲰ
ⲀⲔϮϨⲈ ' ⲈⲂⲞⲖ ϨⲚ̅ ⲦⲠⲎⲄⲎ ⲈⲦⲂⲢ̅ⲂⲢⲈ ⲦⲀⲈⲒ ⲀⲚⲞⲔ '
Ⲛ̅ⲦⲀⲈⲒϢⲒⲦⲤ̅

ⲀⲨⲰ ⲀϤϪⲒⲦϤ̅ ⲀϤⲀⲚⲀⲬⲰⲢⲈⲒ ' ⲀϤϪⲰ ⲚⲀϤ
Ⲛ̅ϢⲞⲘⲦ Ⲛ̅ϢⲀϪⲈ

Ⲛ̅ⲦⲀⲢⲈⲐⲰ̔ⲘⲀⲤ ϪⲈ ⲈⲒ ϢⲀ ⲚⲈϤϢⲂⲈⲈⲢ ⲀⲨϪⲚⲞⲨϤ
ϪⲈ [10] Ⲛ̅ⲦⲀⲒⲥ̅ ϪⲞⲞⲤ ϪⲈ ⲞⲨ ⲚⲀⲔ

ΠⲈϪⲀϤ ⲚⲀⲨ Ⲛ̅ϬⲒ ' ⲐⲰⲘⲀⲤ ϪⲈ ⲈⲒϢⲀⲚϪⲰ
ⲚⲎⲦⲚ̅ ⲞⲨⲀ ϨⲚ̅ Ⲛ̅ϢⲀ̔ϪⲈ Ⲛ̅ⲦⲀϤϪⲞⲞⲨ ⲚⲀⲈⲒ
ⲦⲈⲦⲚⲀϤⲒ ⲰⲚⲈ Ⲛ̅ⲦⲈ̔ⲦⲚ̅ⲚⲞⲨϪⲈ ⲈⲢⲞⲈⲒ ⲀⲨⲰ
Ⲛ̅ⲦⲈⲞⲨⲔⲰϨⲦ ⲈⲒ Ⲉ̔ⲂⲞⲖ ϨⲚ̅ Ⲛ̅ⲰⲚⲈ Ⲛ̅ⲤⲢⲰϨⲔ Ⲙ̅ⲘⲰⲦⲚ̅

14 ΠⲈϪⲈ [15] ⲓ̅ⲥ̅ ⲚⲀⲨ ϪⲈ ⲈⲦⲈⲦⲚ̅ϢⲀⲚⲢ̅ⲚⲎⲤⲦⲈⲨⲈ
ⲦⲈⲦⲚⲀ̔ϪⲠⲞ ⲚⲎⲦⲚ̅ Ⲛ̅ⲞⲨⲚⲞⲂⲈ ⲀⲨⲰ
ⲈⲦⲈⲦⲚ̅ϢⲀⲚϢⲖⲎⲖ ⲤⲈⲚⲀⲢ̅ⲔⲀⲦⲀⲔⲢⲒⲚⲈ Ⲙ̅ⲘⲰⲦⲚ̅ ⲀⲨⲰ
' ⲈⲦⲈⲦⲚ̅ϢⲀⲚϮ ⲈⲖⲈⲎⲘⲞⲤⲨⲚⲎ ⲈⲦⲈⲦⲚⲀⲈⲒ̔ⲢⲈ
Ⲛ̅ⲞⲨⲔⲀⲔⲞⲚ Ⲛ̅ⲚⲈⲦⲘ̅Ⲡⲛ̅Ⲁ

ⲀⲨⲰ ⲈⲦⲈⲦⲚ̅ [20] ϢⲀⲚⲂⲰⲔ ⲈϨⲞⲨⲚ ⲈⲔⲀϨ ⲚⲒⲘ ⲀⲨⲰ
Ⲛ̅ⲦⲈⲦⲘ̅ⲘⲞⲞϢⲈ ϨⲚ̅ Ⲛ̅ⲬⲰⲢⲀ ⲈⲨϢⲀⲢ̅ⲠⲀⲢⲀⲆⲈⲬⲈ '
Ⲙ̅ⲘⲰⲦⲚ̅ ⲠⲈⲦⲞⲨⲚⲀⲔⲀⲀⲨ ϨⲀⲢⲰⲦⲚ̅ ⲞⲨⲞⲘϤ̅ '
ⲚⲈⲦϢⲰⲚⲈ Ⲛ̅ϨⲎⲦⲞⲨ ⲈⲢⲒ̔ⲐⲈⲢⲀⲠⲈⲨⲈ Ⲙ̅ⲘⲞ̔ⲞⲨ
ⲠⲈⲦⲚⲀⲂⲰⲔ ⲄⲀⲢ ⲈϨⲞⲨⲚ ϨⲚ̅ ⲦⲈⲦⲚ̅ⲦⲀ[25]ⲠⲢⲞ
ϤⲚⲀϪⲰϨⲘ̅ ⲦⲎⲨⲦⲚ̅ ⲀⲚ ⲀⲖⲖⲀ ⲠⲈⲦⲚ̅ⲚⲎⲨ ⲈⲂⲞⲖ ϨⲚ̅
ⲦⲈⲦⲚ̅ⲦⲀⲠⲢⲞ Ⲛ̅ⲦⲞϤ ⲠⲈ̔ⲦⲚⲀϪⲀϨⲘ̅ ⲦⲎⲨⲦⲚ̅

13   Jesus said to his followers, "Compare me to something and tell me what I am like."

Simon Peter said to him, "You are like a just messenger."

Matthew said to him, "You are like a wise philosopher."

Thomas said to him, "Teacher, my mouth is utterly unable to say what you are like."

Jesus said, "I am not your teacher. Because you have drunk, you have become intoxicated from the bubbling spring that I have tended."

And he took him, and withdrew, and spoke three sayings to him.

When Thomas came back to his friends, they asked him, "What did Jesus say to you?"

Thomas said to them, "If I tell you one of the sayings he spoke to me, you will pick up rocks and stone me, and fire will come from the rocks and consume you."

14   Jesus said to them, "If you fast, you will bring sin upon yourselves, and if you pray, you will be condemned, and if you give to charity, you will harm your spirits.

"When you go into any region and walk through the countryside, when people receive you, eat what they serve you and heal the sick among them. For what goes into your mouth will not defile you; rather, it is what comes out of your mouth that will defile you."

15 ΠΕΧΕ Ι̅С̅ ΔΕ ϩΟΤΑΝ ' ΕΤΕΤΝ̅ϢΑΝΝΑΥ ΕΠΕΤΕ
Μ̅ΠΟΥΧΠΟΥ ' ΕΒΟΛ ϩΝ̅ ΤϹϩΙΜΕ ΠΕϩΤ ΤΗΥΤΝ̅ ΕΧΜ̅
[30] ΠΕΤΝ̅ϩΟ Ν̅ΤΕΤΝ̅ΟΥⲰϢΤ ΝΑϤ ΠΕΤΜ̅ΜΑΥ ΠΕ
ΠΕΤΝ̅ΕΙⲰΤ

16 ΠΕΧΕ Ι̅С̅ ΔΕ ΤΑΧΑ ' ΕΥΜΕΕΥΕ Ν̅ϬΙ Ρ̅ΡⲰΜΕ ΔΕ
Ν̅ΤΑΕΙΕΙ ΕΝΟΥΧΕ Ν̅ΟΥΕΙΡΗΝΗ ΕΧΜ̅ ΠΚΟСΜΟС
ΑΥⲰ ' СΕСΟΟΥΝ ΑΝ ΔΕ Ν̅ΤΑΕΙΕΙ ΑΝΟΥΧΕ
Ν̅ϩΝ̅[35]ΠⲰΡΧ ΕΧΝ̅ ΠΚΑϩ ΟΥΚⲰϩΤ ΟΥСΗϤΕ '
ΟΥΠΟΛΕΜΟС ΟΥΝ̅ ϮΟΥ ΓΑΡ ΝΑϢⲰΠΕ 3 6ϩΝ̅
ΟΥΗΕΙ ΟΥΝ̅ ϢΟΜΤ ΝΑϢⲰΠΕ ΕΧΝ̅ ' СΝΑΥ ΑΥⲰ
СΝΑΥ ΕΧΝ̅ ϢΟΜΤ ΠΕΙⲰΤ ' ΕΧΜ̅ ΠϢΗΡΕ ΑΥⲰ
ΠϢΗΡΕ ΕΧΜ̅ ΠΕΙⲰΤ ' ΑΥⲰ СΕΝΑⲰϩΕ ΕΡΑΤΟΥ ΕΥΟ
Μ̅ΜΟΝΑ[5]ΧΟС

17 ΠΕΧΕ Ι̅С̅ ΔΕ ϮΝΑϮ ΝΗΤΝ̅ Μ̅ΠΕΤΕ ' Μ̅ΠΕΒΑΛ
ΝΑΥ ΕΡΟϤ ΑΥⲰ ΠΕΤΕ Μ̅ΠΕΜΑΑΧΕ СΟΤΜΕϤ ΑΥⲰ
ΠΕΤΕ Μ̅ΠΕϬΙΧ ϬΜ̅ϬⲰΜϤ ΑΥⲰ Μ̅ΠΕϤΕΙ ΕϩΡΑΪ ϩΙ
ΦΗΤ ' Ρ̅ΡⲰΜΕ

18 ΠΕΧΕ Μ̅ΜΑΘΗΤΗС Ν̅ Ι̅С̅ ΔΕ ΧΟ[10]ΟС ΕΡΟΝ ΧΕ
ΤΝ̅ϩΑΗ ΕСΝΑϢⲰΠΕ Ν̅ΑϢ Ν̅ϩΕ
ΠΕΧΕ Ι̅С̅ ΑΤΕΤΝ̅ϬⲰΛΠ ΓΑΡ ΕΒΟΛ ' Ν̅ΤΑΡΧΗ
ΧΕΚΑΑС ΕΤΕΤΝΑϢΙΝΕ Ν̅СΑ ' ΘΑϩΗ ΧΕ ϩΜ̅ ΠΜΑ
ΕΤΕ ΤΑΡΧΗ Μ̅ΜΑΥ ΕΘΑϩΗ ΝΑϢⲰΠΕ Μ̅ΜΑΥ
ΟΥΜΑΚΑΡΙΟС [15] ΠΕΤΝΑⲰϩΕ ΕΡΑΤϤ ϩΝ̅ ΤΑΡΧΗ
ΑΥⲰ ' ϤΝΑСΟΥⲰΝ ΘΑϩΗ ΑΥⲰ ϤΝΑΧΙ ϮΠΕ ' ΑΝ
Μ̅ΜΟΥ

19 ΠΕΧΕ Ι̅С̅ ΔΕ ΟΥΜΑΚΑΡΙΟС ' ΠΕ ΝΤΑϥϢⲰΠΕ ϩΑ
ΤΕϩΗ ΕΜΠΑΤΕϤϢⲰ ' ΠΕ
ΕΤΕΤΝ̅ϢΑΝϢⲰΠΕ ΝΑΕΙ Μ̅ΜΑΘΗ[20]ΤΗС
Ν̅ΤΕΤΝ̅СⲰΤΜ̅ ΑΝΑϢΑΧΕ ΝΕΕΙⲰ ' ΝΕ ΝΑΡ̅ΔΙΑΚΟΝΕΙ
ΝΗΤΝ̅
ΟΥΝ̅ΤΗΤΝ̅ ' ΓΑΡ Μ̅ΜΑΥ Ν̅ϮΟΥ Ν̅ϢΗΝ ϩΜ̅
ΠΑΡΑ ' ΔΙСΟС ΕСΕΚΙΜ ΑΝ Ν̅ϢⲰΜ Μ̅ΠΡⲰ ' ΑΥⲰ
ΜΑΡΕΝΟΥϬⲰΒΕ ϩΕ ΕΒΟΛ ΠΕΤ[25]ΝΑСΟΥⲰΝΟΥ
ϤΝΑΧΙ ϮΠΕ ΑΝ Μ̅ΜΟΥ '

15   Jesus said, "When you see one who was not born of woman, fall on your faces and worship. That is your father."

16   Jesus said, "Perhaps people think that I have come to impose peace upon the world. They do not know that I have come to impose conflicts upon the earth: fire, sword, war. For there will be five in a house: There will be three against two and two against three, father against son and son against father, and they will stand alone."

17   Jesus said, "I shall give you what no eye has seen, what no ear has heard, what no hand has touched, what has not arisen in the human heart."

18   The followers said to Jesus, "Tell us how our end will be."

Jesus said, "Have you discovered the beginning, then, so that you are seeking the end? For where the beginning is, the end will be. Fortunate is one who stands at the beginning: That one will know the end and will not taste death."

19   Jesus said, "Fortunate is one who came into being before coming into being.

"If you become my followers and listen to my sayings, these stones will serve you.

"For there are five trees in paradise for you; they do not change, summer or winter, and their leaves do not fall. Whoever knows them will not taste death."

20   ⲡⲉϪⲉ ⲙ̅ⲙⲁⲑⲏⲧⲏⲥ ⲛ̅ⲓ̅ⲥ̅ Ϫⲉ Ϫⲟⲟⲥ 'ⲉⲣⲟⲛ Ϫⲉ
ⲧⲙ̅ⲛ̅ⲧⲉⲣⲟ ⲛ̅ⲙ̅ⲡⲏⲩⲉ ⲉⲥ'ⲧ̅ⲛ̅ⲧⲱⲛ ⲉⲛⲓⲙ

ⲡⲉϪⲁⲩ ⲛⲁⲩ Ϫⲉ ⲉⲥⲧ̅ⲛ̅ⲧⲱⲛ ⲁⲩⲃ̅ⲗ̅ⲃⲓⲗⲉ ⲛ̅ϣ̅ⲗ̅ⲧⲁⲙ
‹ⲥ›ⲥⲟⲃ̅ⲕ̅ ⲡⲁ³⁰ⲣⲁ ⲛ̅ϭⲣⲟϭ ⲧⲏⲣⲟⲩ ϩⲟⲧⲁⲛ Ϫⲉ
ⲉⲥϣⲁⲛ'ϩⲉ ⲉϪ̅ⲙ̅ ⲡⲕⲁϩ ⲉⲧⲟⲩⲣ̅ ϩⲱⲃ ⲉⲣⲟⲥ
ϣⲁⲩ'ⲧⲉⲩⲟ ⲉⲃⲟⲗ ⲛ̅ⲛⲟⲩⲛⲟϭ ⲛ̅ⲧⲁⲣ ⲛ̅ⲩϣⲱⲡⲉ
ⲛ̅ⲥⲕⲉⲡⲏ ⲛ̅ϩⲁⲗⲁⲧⲉ ⲛ̅ⲧⲡⲉ

21   ⲡⲉ'Ϫⲉ ⲙⲁⲣⲓϩⲁⲙ ⲛ̅ⲓ̅ⲥ̅ Ϫⲉ ⲉⲛⲉⲕⲙⲁⲑⲏ³⁵ⲧⲏⲥ
ⲉⲓⲛⲉ ⲛ̅ⲛⲓⲙ

ⲡⲉϪⲁⲩ Ϫⲉ ⲉⲩⲉⲓⲛⲉ 37 ⲛ̅ϩ̅ⲛ̅ϣⲏⲣⲉ ϣⲏⲙ ⲉⲩϭⲉⲗⲓⲧ
ⲁⲩⲥⲱϣⲉ ⲉⲧⲱⲟⲩ ⲁⲛ ⲧⲉ ϩⲟⲧⲁⲛ ⲉⲩϣⲁⲉⲓ ⲛ̅ϭⲓ
ⲛ̅Ϫⲟⲉⲓⲥ 'ⲛ̅ⲧⲥⲱϣⲉ ⲥⲉⲛⲁϪⲟⲟⲥ Ϫⲉ ⲕⲉ ⲧⲛ̅ⲥⲱϣⲉ '
ⲉⲃⲟⲗ ⲛⲁⲛ ⲛ̅ⲧⲟⲟⲩ ⲥⲉⲕⲁⲕ ⲁϩⲏⲩ ⲙ̅ⲡⲟⲩⲙ̅⁵ⲧⲟ ⲉⲃⲟⲗ
ⲉⲧⲣⲟⲩⲕⲁⲁⲥ ⲉⲃⲟⲗ ⲛⲁⲩ ⲛ̅ⲥⲉϯ ⲧⲟⲩ'ⲥⲱϣⲉ ⲛⲁⲩ

ⲇⲓⲁ ⲧⲟⲩⲧⲟ ϯϪⲱ ⲙ̅ⲙⲟⲥ Ϫⲉ ⲉⲩϣⲁⲉⲓⲙⲉ ⲛ̅ϭⲓ
ⲡϪⲉⲥϩⲛ̅ⲏⲉⲓ Ϫⲉ ⲩⲛⲏⲩ ⲛ̅ϭⲓ 'ⲡⲣⲉⲩϪⲓⲟⲩⲉ
ⲩⲛⲁⲣⲟⲉⲓⲥ ⲉⲙⲡⲁⲧⲉⲩⲉⲓ ⲛ̅ⲩⲧⲙ̅ⲕⲁⲁⲩ ⲉϣⲟϪⲧ
ⲉϩⲟⲩⲛ ⲉⲡⲉⲩⲏⲉⲓ ⲛ̅ⲧⲉ ⲧⲉⲩ¹⁰ⲙ̅ⲛ̅ⲧⲉⲣⲟ ⲉⲧⲣⲉⲩϥⲓ
ⲛ̅ⲛⲉⲩⲥⲕⲉⲩⲟⲥ ⲛ̅ⲧⲱⲧ̅ⲛ̅ ' ⲇⲉ ⲣⲟⲉⲓⲥ ϩⲁ ⲧⲉϩⲏ
ⲙ̅ⲡⲕⲟⲥⲙⲟⲥ ⲙⲟⲩⲣ ⲙ̅ⲙⲱⲧ̅ⲛ̅ ⲉϪ̅ⲛ̅ ⲛⲉⲧⲛ̅ϯⲡⲉ
ϩⲛ̅ⲛⲟⲩⲛⲟϭ ⲛ̅ⲇⲩ'ⲛⲁⲙⲓⲥ ϣⲓⲛⲁ Ϫⲉ ⲛⲉⲛⲗⲏⲥⲧⲏⲥ
ϩⲉ ⲉϩⲓⲏ ⲉⲉⲓ 'ϣⲁⲣⲱⲧ̅ⲛ̅ ⲉⲡⲉⲓ ⲧⲉⲭⲣⲉⲓⲁ ⲉⲧⲉⲧⲛ̅ϭⲱϣⲧ
¹⁵ⲉⲃⲟⲗ ϩⲏⲧ̅ⲥ̅ ⲥⲉⲛⲁϩⲉ ⲉⲣⲟⲥ ⲙⲁⲣⲉⲩϣⲱⲡⲉ 'ϩⲛ̅
ⲧⲉⲧⲛ̅ⲙⲏⲧⲉ ⲛ̅ϭⲓ ⲟⲩⲣⲱⲙⲉ ⲛ̅ⲉⲡⲓⲥⲧⲏ'ⲙⲱⲛ

ⲛ̅ⲧⲁⲣⲉⲡⲕⲁⲣⲡⲟⲥ ⲡⲱϩ ⲁϥⲉⲓ ϩⲛ̅ⲛⲟⲩ'ϭⲉⲡⲏ
ⲉⲡⲉϥⲁⲥϩ ϩⲛ̅ ⲧⲉϥϭⲓϪ ⲁϥϩⲁⲥϥ ⲡⲉⲧⲉ ⲟⲩⲛ̅
ⲙⲁⲁϪⲉ ⲙ̅ⲙⲟϥ ⲉⲥⲱⲧ̅ⲙ̅ ⲙⲁⲣⲉϥⲥⲱⲧ̅ⲙ̅ 20

20 The followers said to Jesus, "Tell us what heaven's kingdom is like."

He said to them, "It is like a mustard seed. <It> is the smallest of all seeds, but when it falls on prepared soil, it produces a large plant and becomes a shelter for birds of heaven."

21 Mary said to Jesus, "What are your followers like?"

He said, "They are like little children living in a field that is not theirs. When the owners of the field come, they will say, 'Give our field back to us.' They take off their clothes in front of them in order to give it back to them, and they return their field to them.

"For this reason I say, if the owner of a house knows that a thief is coming, he will be on guard before the thief arrives and will not let the thief break into the house of his estate and steal his possessions. As for you, then, be on guard against the world. Arm yourselves with great strength, or the robbers might find a way to get to you, for the trouble you expect will come. Let there be among you a person who understands.

"When the crop ripened, the person came quickly with sickle in hand and harvested it. Whoever has ears to hear should hear."

22 ⲁ̄ⲓ̅ⲥ̅ ⲛⲁⲩ ⲁ⳿ⲛ̄ⲕⲟⲧⲉⲓ ⲉⲧϫⲓ ⲉⲣⲱⲧⲉ ⲡⲉϫⲁϥ
ⲛ̄ⲛⲉϥⲙⲁⲑⲏⲧⲏⲥ ϫⲉ ⲛⲉⲉⲓⲕⲟⲧⲉⲓ ⲉⲧϫⲓ ⲉⲣⲱ⳿ⲧⲉ
ⲉⲩⲧⲛ̄ⲧⲱⲛ ⲁⲛⲉⲧⲃⲏⲕ ⲉϩⲟⲩⲛ ⲁⲧⲙ̄ⲛ̄ⲧⲉⲣⲟ

ⲡⲉϫⲁⲩ ⲛⲁⲩ ϫⲉ ⲉⲉⲓⲉⲛⲟ ⲛ̄ⲕⲟⲧⲉⲓ ⲧⲛ̄ⲛⲁⲃⲱⲕ
ⲉϩⲟⲩⲛ ⲉⲧⲙ̄ⲛ̄ⲧⲉⲣⲟ

ⲡⲉϫⲉ ⲓ̅ⲏ̅ⲥ̅ ⲛⲁⲩ 25 ϫⲉ ϩⲟⲧⲁⲛ ⲉⲧⲉⲧⲛ̄ϣⲁⲣ̄
ⲡⲥⲛⲁⲩ ⲟⲩⲁ ⲁⲩⲱ ⲉ⳿ⲧⲉⲧⲛ̄ϣⲁⲣ̄ ⲡⲥⲁ ⲛϩⲟⲩⲛ ⲛ̄ⲑⲉ
ⲙ̄ⲡⲥⲁ ⲛⲃⲟⲗ ⲁⲩⲱ ⲡⲥⲁ ⲛⲃⲟⲗ ⲛ̄ⲑⲉ ⲙ̄ⲡⲥⲁ ⲛϩⲟⲩⲛ
ⲁⲩⲱ ⲡⲥⲁ ⲛ⳿ⲧⲡⲉ ⲛ̄ⲑⲉ ⲙ̄ⲡⲥⲁ ⲙⲡⲓⲧⲛ̄ ⲁⲩⲱ ϣⲓⲛⲁ
ⲉⲧⲉ⳿ⲧⲛⲁⲉⲓⲣⲉ ⲙ̄ⲫⲟⲟⲩⲧ ⲙ̄ⲛ̄ ⲧⲥϩⲓⲙⲉ ⲙ̄ⲡⲓⲟⲩⲁ 30
ⲟⲩⲱⲧ ϫⲉⲕⲁⲁⲥ ⲛⲉⲫⲟⲟⲩⲧ ⲣ̄ ϩⲟⲟⲩⲧ ⲛ̄ⲧⲉ⳿ⲧⲥϩⲓⲙⲉ ⲣ̄
ⲥϩⲓⲙⲉ ϩⲟⲧⲁⲛ ⲉⲧⲉⲧⲛ̄ϣⲁⲉⲓⲣⲉ ⳿ⲛϩ̄ⲛⲃⲁⲗ ⲉⲡⲙⲁ
ⲛ̄ⲟⲩⲃⲁⲗ ⲁⲩⲱ ⲟⲩϭⲓϫ ⳿ⲉⲡⲙⲁ ⲛ̄ⲛⲟⲩϭⲓϫ ⲁⲩⲱ
ⲟⲩⲉⲣⲏⲧⲉ ⲉⲡⲙⲁ ⳿ⲛ̄ⲟⲩⲉⲣⲏⲧⲉ ⲟⲩϩⲓⲕⲱⲛ ⲉⲡⲙⲁ
ⲛ̄ⲟⲩϩⲓⲕⲱⲛ 35 ⲧⲟⲧⲉ ⲧⲉⲧⲛⲁⲃⲱⲕ ⲉϩⲟⲩⲛ
ⲉ[ⲧ]ⲙ̄ⲛ̄[ⲧⲉⲣ]ⲟ 38

23 ⲡⲉϫⲉ ⲓ̅ⲥ̅ ϫⲉ ϯⲛⲁⲥⲉⲧⲡ ⲧⲏⲛⲉ ⲟⲩⲁ ⲉⲃⲟⲗ ⳿ϩ̄ⲛ
ϣⲟ ⲁⲩⲱ ⲥⲛⲁⲩ ⲉⲃⲟⲗ ϩ̄ⲛ ⲧⲃⲁ ⲁⲩⲱ ⳿ⲥⲉⲛⲁⲱϩⲉ
ⲉⲣⲁⲧⲟⲩ ⲉⲩⲟ ⲟⲩⲁ ⲟⲩⲱⲧ

24 ⲡⲉ⳿ϫⲉ ⲛⲉϥⲙⲁⲑⲏⲧⲏⲥ ϫⲉ ⲙⲁⲧⲥⲉⲃⲟⲛ ⲉⲡⲧⲟ⁵ⲡⲟⲥ
ⲉⲧⲕⲙ̄ⲙⲁⲩ ⲉⲡⲉⲓ ⲧⲁⲛⲁⲅⲕⲏ ⲉⲣⲟⲛ ⲧⲉ ⳿ⲉⲧⲣⲛ̄ϣⲓⲛⲉ
ⲛ̄ⲥⲱϥ

ⲡⲉϫⲁϥ ⲛⲁⲩ ϫⲉ ⲡⲉⲧⲉⲩⲧ⳿ⲛ̄ ⲙⲁⲁϫⲉ ⲙ̄ⲙⲟϥ
ⲙⲁⲣⲉϥⲥⲱⲧⲙ̄ ⲟⲩⲛ̄ ⲟⲩ⳿ⲟⲉⲓⲛ ϣⲟⲟⲡ ⲙ̄ⲫⲟⲩⲛ
ⲛ̄ⲛⲟⲩⲣⲙ̄ⲟⲩⲟⲉⲓⲛ ⳿ⲁⲩⲱ ϥⲣ̄ ⲟⲩⲟⲉⲓⲛ ⲉⲡⲕⲟⲥⲙⲟⲥ
ⲧⲏⲣϥ ⲉϥⲧⲙ̄¹⁰ⲣ̄ ⲟⲩⲟⲉⲓⲛ ⲟⲩⲕⲁⲕⲉ ⲡⲉ

25 ⲡⲉϫⲉ ⲓ̅ⲥ̅ ϫⲉ ⲙⲉⲣⲉ ⳿ⲡⲉⲕⲥⲟⲛ ⲛ̄ⲑⲉ ⲛ̄ⲧⲉⲕⲯⲩⲭⲏ
ⲉⲣⲓⲧⲏⲣⲉⲓ ⲙ̄ⲙⲟϥ ⳿ⲛ̄ⲑⲉ ⲛ̄ⲧⲉⲗⲟⲩ ⲙ̄ⲡⲉⲕⲃⲁⲗ

26 ⲡⲉϫⲉ ⲓ̅ⲥ̅ ϫⲉ ⲡϫⲏ ⳿ⲉⲧϩ̄ⲙ ⲡⲃⲁⲗ ⲙ̄ⲡⲉⲕⲥⲟⲛ
ⲕⲛⲁⲩ ⲉⲣⲟϥ ⲡⲥⲟⲉⲓ ⳿ⲇⲉ ⲉⲧϩ̄ⲙ ⲡⲉⲕⲃⲁⲗ ⲕⲛⲁⲩ ⲁ⳿.
ⲉⲣⲟϥ ϩⲟⲧⲁⲛ 15 ⲉⲕϣⲁⲛⲛⲟⲩϫⲉ ⲙ̄ⲡⲥⲟⲉⲓ ⲉⲃⲟ⳿ⲗ ϩ̄ⲙ
ⲡⲉⲕ⳿ⲃⲁⲗ ⲧⲟⲧⲉ ⲕⲛⲁⲛⲁⲩ ⲉⲃⲟⲗ ⲉⲛⲟⲩϫⲉ ⲙ̄ⲡϫⲏ ⳿
ⲉⲃⲟⲗ ϩ̄ⲙ ⲡⲃⲁⲗ ⲙ̄ⲡⲉⲕⲥⲟⲛ

22   Jesus saw some babies nursing. He said to his followers, "These nursing babies are like those who enter the kingdom."

They said to him, "Then shall we enter the kingdom as babies?"

Jesus said to them, "When you make the two into one, and when you make the inner like the outer and the outer like the inner, and the upper like the lower, and when you make male and female into a single one, so that the male will not be male nor the female be female, when you make eyes in place of an eye, a hand in place of a hand, a foot in place of a foot, an image in place of an image, then you will enter [the kingdom]."

23   Jesus said, "I shall choose you, one from a thousand and two from ten thousand, and they will stand as a single one."

24   His followers said, "Show us the place where you are, for we must seek it."

He said to them, "Whoever has ears should hear. There is light within a person of light, and it shines on the whole world. If it does not shine, it is dark."

25   Jesus said, "Love your brother like your soul, protect that person like the pupil of your eye."

26   Jesus said, "You see the speck that is in your brother's eye, but you do not see the beam that is in your own eye. When you take the beam out of your own eye, then you will see clearly to take the speck out of your brother's eye.

27 ετε‹ΤΝ›ΤΜ̄ΡΝΗΪCΤΕΥΕ ΕΠΚΟCΜΟC ΤΕΤΝΑϩΕ ΑΝ
ΕΤΜ̄ΝΤΕΙΡΟ ΕΤΕΤΝ̄ΤΜ̄ΕΙΡΕ Μ̄ΠCΑΜΒΑΤΟΝ
Ν̄CΑΒ²⁰ΒΑΤΟΝ Ν̄ΤΕΤΝΑΝΑΥ ΑΝ ΕΠΕΙⲰΤ

28 ΠΕϪΕ Ι̅C̅ ϪΕ ΑΕΙⲰϩΕ ΕΡΑΤ ϩΝ̄ ΤΜΗΤΕ
Μ̄ΠΚΟCΜΟC ΑΥⲰ ΑΕΙΟΥⲰΝϩ ΕΒΟΛ ΝΑΥ ϩΝ̄ CΑΡϪ
ΪΑΕΙϩΕ ΕΡΟΟΥ ΤΗΡΟΥ ΕΥΤΑϩΕ Μ̄ΠΙϩΕ ΕΛΑΪΑΥ
Ν̄ϨΗΤΟΥ ΕϤΟΒΕ ΑΥⲰ ΑΤΑΨΥΧΗ † ΤΚΑC ²⁵ΕϪΝ̄
Ν̄ϢΗΡΕ Ν̄ΡΡⲰΜΕ ϪΕ ϩΝ̄ΒⲖⲖΕΕΥΕ ΝΕ ϩΜ̄ ΠΟΥϩΗΤ
ΑΥⲰ CΕΝΑΥ ΕΒΟⲖ ΑΝ ΪϪΕ Ν̄ΤΑΥΕΙ ΕΠΚΟCΜΟC
ΕΥϢΟΥΕΙΤ ΕΥϢΙΝΕ ΟΝ ΕΤΡΟΥΕΙ ΕΒΟⲖ ϩΜ̄
ΠΚΟCΜΟC ΪΕΥϢΟΥΕΙΤ ΠⲖΗΝ ΤΕΝΟΥ CΕΤΟϩΕ
ϩΟ³⁰ΤΑΝ ΕΥϢΑΝΝΕϩ ΠΟΥΗΡΠ ΤΟΤΕ
CΕΝΑΡ̄ΪΜΕΤΑΝΟΕΙ

29 ΠΕϪΕ Ι̅C̅ ΕϢϪΕ Ν̄ΤΑΤCΑΡϪ ΪϢⲰΠΕ ΕΤΒΕ ΠΝ̄Ᾱ
ΟΥϢΠΗΡΕ ΤΕ ΕϢΪϪΕ ΠΝ̄Ᾱ ϪΕ ΕΤΒΕ ΠCⲰΜΑ
ΟΥϢΠΗΡΕ ΪΝ̄ϢΠΗΡΕ ΠΕ ΑⲖⲖΑ ΑΝΟΚ †Ρ̄ ϢΠΗΡΕ
39 Μ̄ΠΑΕΙ ϪΕ ΠⲰС ΑΤΕ̣ΕΙΝΟϬ Μ̄Μ̄Ν̄ΤΡΜ̄ΜΑΪΟ
ΑCΟΥⲰϩ ϩΝ̄ ΤΕΕΙΜ̄ΝΤϨΗΚΕ

30 ΠΕϪΕ Ι̅C̅ ΪϪΕ ΠΜΑ ΕΥΝ̄ ϢΟΜΤ Ν̄ΝΟΥΤΕ Μ̄ΜΑΥ
ϩΝ̄ΪΝΟΥΤΕ ΝΕ ΠΜΑ ΕΥΝ̄ CΝΑΥ Η ΟΥΑ ΑΝΟΚ ⁵
†ϢΟΟΠ ΝΜΜΑϤ

31 ΠΕϪΕ Ι̅C̅ ΜΝ̄ ΠΡΟΦΗΪΤΗC ϢΗΠ ϩΜ̄ ΠΕϤΤΜΕ
ΜΑΡΕCΟΕΙΝ Ρ̄Θ̣ΕΪΡΑΠΕΥΕ Ν̄ΝΕΤCΟΟΥΝ Μ̄ΜΟϤ

32 ΠΕϪΕ Ι̅C̅ ΪϪΕ ΟΥΠΟΛΙC ΕΥΚⲰΤ Μ̄ΜΟC ϩΙϪΝ̄
ΟΥΤΟΪΟΥ ΕϤϪΟCΕ ΕCΤΑϪΡΗΥ ΜΝ̄ ϬΟΜ Ν̄CϩΕ ¹⁰
ΟΥϪΕ CΝΑϢϩⲰΠ ΑΝ

33 ΠΕϪΕ Ι̅C̅ ΠΕΤΚΝΑΪCⲰΤΜ̄ ΕΡΟϤ ϩΜ̄ ΠΕΚΜΑΑϪΕ
ϩΜ̄ ΠΚΕΜΑΪΑϪΕ ΤΑϢΕ ΟΕΙϢ Μ̄ΜΟϤ ϩΙϪΝ̄
ΝΕΤΝ̄ϪΕΪΝΕΠⲰΡ ΜΑΡΕⲖΑΑΥ ϬΑΡ ϪΕΡΕ ϩΗΒ̄C̄
Ν̄ϤΪΚΑΑϤ ϩΑ ΜΑΑϪΕ ΟΥϪΕ ΜΑϤΚΑΑϤ ϩΜ̄ ΜΑ ¹⁵
ΕϤϨΗΠ ΑⲖⲖΑ ΕϢΑΡΕϤΚΑΑϤ ϩΙϪΝ̄ ΤⲖΥΪΧΝΙΑ
ϪΕΚΑΑC ΟΥΟΝ ΝΙΜ ΕΤΒΗΚ ΕϨΟΥΝ ΪΑΥⲰ ΕΤΝ̄ΝΗΥ
ΕΒΟⲖ ΕΥΝΑΥ ΑΠΕϤΟΥΟΕΙΝ

27   "If you do not fast from the world, you will not find the kingdom. If you do not observe the sabbath as a sabbath, you will not see the father."

28   Jesus said, "I took my stand in the midst of the world, and in flesh I appeared to them. I found them all drunk, and I did not find any of them thirsty. My soul ached for the children of humanity, because they are blind in their hearts and do not see, for they came into the world empty, and they also seek to depart from the world empty. But now they are drunk. When they shake off their wine, then they will repent."

29   Jesus said, "If the flesh came into being because of spirit, it is a marvel, but if spirit came into being because of the body, it is a marvel of marvels. Yet I marvel at how this great wealth has come to dwell in this poverty."

30   Jesus said, "Where there are three deities, they are divine. Where there are two or one, I am with that one."

31   Jesus said, "A prophet is not acceptable in the prophet's own town; a doctor does not heal those who know the doctor."

32   Jesus said, "A city built upon a high hill and fortified cannot fall, nor can it be hidden."

33   Jesus said, "What you will hear in your ear, in the other ear proclaim from your rooftops. For no one lights a lamp and puts it under a basket, nor does one put it in a hidden place. Rather, one puts it on a stand so that all who come and go will see its light."

34 ΠΕϪΕ ΙC ϪΕ ΟⲨΒⲖⲖΕ ΕϤϢⲀⲚCⲰΚ ' ϩΗΤϤ
ⲚⲚΟⲨΒⲖⲖΕ ϢⲀⲨϩΕ ⲘⲠΕCⲚⲀⲨ 20 ΕΠΕCΗΤ ΕⲨϩΙΕΙⲦ

35 ΠΕϪΕ ΙC ⲘⲚ ϬΟⲘ ' ⲚⲦΕΟⲨⲀ ΒⲰΚ ΕϩΟⲨⲚ ΕΠΗΕΙ
ⲘΠϪⲰⲰⲢΕ ⲚϤϪΙⲦϤ ⲚϪⲚⲀϩ ΕΙ ΜΗΤΙ ⲚϤⲘΟⲨⲢ '
ⲚⲚΕϤϬΙϪ ⲦΟⲦΕ ϤⲚⲀΠⲰⲚΕ ΕΒΟⲖ ' ⲘΠΕϤΗΕΙ

36 ΠΕϪΕ ΙC ⲘⲚϤΙ ⲢΟΟⲨϢ ϪΙⲚ 25 ϩⲦΟΟⲨΕ ϢⲀ
ⲢΟⲨϩΕ ⲀⲨⲰ ϪΙⲚ ϩΙⲢΟⲨϩΕ ' ϢⲀ ϩⲦΟΟⲨΕ ϪΕ ΟⲨ
ΠΕ<Ⲧ>ΕⲦⲚⲀⲦⲀⲀϤ ϩΙⲰⲦ'ⲦΗⲨⲦⲚ

37 ΠΕϪΕ ⲚΕϤⲘⲀΘΗⲦΗC ϪΕ ⲀϢ Ⲛ'ϩΟΟⲨ
ΕΚⲚⲀΟⲨⲰⲚϩ ΕΒΟⲖ ⲚⲀⲚ ⲀⲨⲰ ⲀϢ ' Ⲛϩ'ΟΟⲨ
ΕⲚⲀⲚⲀⲨ ΕⲢΟΚ

ΠΕϪΕ ΙC ϪΕ ϩΟ30ⲦⲀⲚ ΕⲦΕⲦⲚϢⲀΚΕΚ ⲦΗⲨⲦⲚ
ΕϩΗⲨ ⲘΠΕ'ⲦⲚϢΙΠΕ ⲀⲨⲰ ⲚⲦΕⲦⲚϤΙ ⲚⲚΕⲦⲚϢⲦΗⲚ '
ⲚⲦΕⲦⲚΚⲀⲀⲨ ϩⲀ ΠΕCΗⲦ ⲚⲚΕⲦⲚΟⲨΕⲢΗ'ⲦΕ ⲚΘΕ
ⲚⲚΙΚΟⲨΕΙ ⲚϢΗⲢΕ ϢΗⲘ ⲚⲦΕ'ⲦⲚϪΟΠϪⲠ ⲘⲘΟΟⲨ
ⲦΟⲦΕ [ⲦΕⲦ]ⲚⲀⲚⲀⲨ 40 ΕΠϢΗⲢΕ ⲘΠΕⲦΟⲚϩ ⲀⲨⲰ
ⲦΕⲦⲚⲀⲢ'ϩΟⲦΕ ⲀⲚ

38 ΠΕϪΕ ΙC ϪΕ ϩⲀϩ ⲚCΟΠ ⲀⲦΕⲦⲚⲢ'ΕΠΙΘⲨⲘΕΙ
ΕCⲰⲦⲘ ⲀⲚΕΕΙϢⲀϪΕ ⲚⲀΕΙ ' Ε⳦ϪⲰ ⲘⲘΟΟⲨ ⲚΗⲦⲚ
ⲀⲨⲰ ⲘⲚⲦΗⲦⲚ 5 ΚΕΟⲨⲀ ΕCΟⲦⲘΟⲨ ⲚⲦΟΟⲦϤ ΟⲨⲚ
ϩⲚϩΟ'ΟⲨ ⲚⲀϢⲰΠΕ ⲚⲦΕⲦⲚϢΙⲚΕ ⲚCⲰΕΙ ⲦΕ'ⲦⲚⲀϩΕ
ⲀⲚ ΕⲢΟΕΙ

39 ΠΕϪΕ ΙC ϪΕ ⲘⲪⲀⲢΙCⲀΙ'ΟC ⲘⲚ ⲚⳤⲢⲀⲘⲘⲀⲦΕⲨC
ⲀⲨϪΙ ⲚϢⲀϢⲦ ' ⲚⲦⳤⲚⲰCΙC ⲀⲨϩΟΠΟⲨ ΟⲨⲦΕ
ⲘΠΟⲨΒⲰΚ 10 ΕϩΟⲨⲚ ⲀⲨⲰ ⲚΕⲦΟⲨⲰϢ ΕΒⲰΚ ΕϩΟⲨⲚ
ⲘΠΟⲨΚⲀⲀⲨ ⲚⲦⲰⲦⲚ ϪΕ ϢⲰΠΕ ⲘⲪⲢΟⲚΙⲘΟC 'ⲚΘΕ
ⲚⲚϩΟϤ ⲀⲨⲰ ⲚⲀΚΕⲢⲀΙΟC ⲚΘΕ ⲚⲚϬⲢΟⲘΠΕ

40 ΠΕϪΕ ΙC ΟⲨΒΕⲚΕⲖΟΟⲖΕ ⲀⲨⲦΟϬC ⲘΠCⲀ ⲚΒΟⲖ
ⲘΠΕΙⲰⲦ ⲀⲨⲰ ΕCⲦⲀ15ϪⲢΗⲨ ⲀⲚ CΕⲚⲀΠΟⲢΚⳞ ϩⲀ
ⲦΕCⲚΟⲨⲚΕ ⲚC'ⲦⲀΚΟ

41 ΠΕϪΕ ΙC ϪΕ ΠΕⲦΕⲨⲚⲦⲀϤ ϩⲚ ⲦΕϤϬΙϪ CΕⲚⲀϮ
ⲚⲀϤ ⲀⲨⲰ ΠΕⲦΕ ⲘⲚⲦⲀϤ ΠΚΕϢΗⲘ ΕⲦΟⲨⲚⲦⲀϤ
CΕⲚⲀϤΙⲦϤ ⲚⲦΟΟⲦϤ '

34   Jesus said, "If a blind person leads a blind person, both of them will fall into a hole."

35   Jesus said, "You cannot enter the house of the strong and take it by force without tying the person's hands. Then you can loot the person's house."

36   Jesus said, "Do not worry, from morning to evening and from evening to morning, about what you will wear."

37   His followers said, "When will you appear to us and when shall we see you?"

Jesus said, "When you strip without being ashamed and you take your clothes and put them under your feet like little children and trample them, then [you] will see the child of the living one and you will not be afraid."

38   Jesus said, "Often you have desired to hear these sayings that I am speaking to you, and you have no one else from whom to hear them. There will be days when you will seek me and you will not find me."

39   Jesus said, "The Pharisees and the scribes have taken the keys of knowledge and have hidden them. They have not entered, nor have they allowed those who want to enter to do so. As for you, be as shrewd as snakes and as innocent as doves."

40   Jesus said, "A grapevine has been planted away from the father. Since it is not strong, it will be pulled up by its root and will perish."

41   Jesus said, "Whoever has something in hand will be given more, and whoever has nothing will be deprived of even the little that person has."

42   ⲡⲉϫⲉ ⲓ̅ⲥ̅ ϫⲉ ϣⲱⲡⲉ ⲉⲧⲉⲧⲛ̅ⲣ̅ⲡⲁⲣⲁⲅⲉ [20]

43   ⲡⲉϫⲁⲩ ⲛⲁϥ ⲛ̅ϭⲓ ⲛⲉϥⲙⲁⲑⲏⲧⲏⲥ ϫⲉ ⲛ̅ⲧⲁⲕ ˈ
ⲛⲓⲙ ⲉⲕϫⲱ ⲛ̅ⲛⲁⲓ̈ ⲛⲁⲛ
ϩⲛ̅ ⲛⲉⲧϫⲱ ⲙ̅ⲙⲟⲟⲩ ⲛⲏⲧⲛ̅ ⲛ̅ⲧⲉⲧⲛ̅ⲉⲓⲙⲉ ⲁⲛ ϫⲉ
ⲁⲛⲟⲕ ˈ ⲛⲓⲙ ⲁⲗⲗⲁ ⲛ̅ⲧⲱⲧⲛ̅ ⲁⲧⲉⲧⲛ̅ϣⲱⲡⲉ ⲛ̅ⲑⲉ
ⲛ̅ⲛⲓ̈ⲟⲩⲇⲁⲓⲟⲥ ϫⲉ ⲥⲉⲙⲉ ⲙ̅ⲡϣⲏⲛ ⲥⲉⲙⲟⲥ [25] ⲧⲉ
ⲙ̅ⲡⲉϥⲕⲁⲣⲡⲟⲥ ⲁⲩⲱ ⲥⲉⲙⲉ ⲙ̅ⲡⲕⲁⲣⲡⲟⲥ ˈ ⲥⲉⲙⲟⲥⲧⲉ
ⲙ̅ⲡϣⲏⲛ

44   ⲡⲉϫⲉ ⲓ̅ⲥ̅ ϫⲉ ⲡⲉⲧⲁϫⲉ ˈ ⲟⲩⲁ ⲁⲡⲉⲓⲱⲧ ⲥⲉⲛⲁⲕⲱ
ⲉⲃⲟⲗ ⲛⲁϥ ⲁⲩⲱ ˈ ⲡⲉⲧⲁϫⲉ ⲟⲩⲁ ⲉⲡϣⲏⲣⲉ ⲥⲉⲛⲁⲕⲱ
ⲉⲃⲟⲗ ˈ ⲛⲁϥ ⲡⲉⲧⲁϫⲉ ⲟⲩⲁ ⲇⲉ ⲁⲡⲡⲛ̅ⲁ̅ ⲉⲧⲟⲩⲁⲁⲃ [30]
ⲥⲉⲛⲁⲕⲱ ⲁⲛ ⲉⲃⲟⲗ ⲛⲁϥ ⲟⲩⲧⲉ ϩⲙ̅ ⲡⲕⲁϩ ˈ ⲟⲩⲧⲉ
ϩⲛ̅ ⲧⲡⲉ

45   ⲡⲉϫⲉ ⲓ̅ⲥ̅ ⲙⲁⲩϫⲉⲗⲉ ⲉⲗⲟⲟˈⲗⲉ ⲉⲃⲟⲗ ϩⲛ̅ ϣⲟⲛⲧⲉ
ⲟⲩⲧⲉ ⲙⲁⲩⲕⲱⲧϥ ˈ ⲕⲛ̅ⲧⲉ ⲉⲃⲟⲗ ϩⲛ̅ ⲥⲣ̅ϭⲁⲙⲟⲩⲗ
ⲙⲁⲩϯ ⲕⲁⲣⲡⲟⲥ ˈ ⲅⲁⲣ ⲟⲩⲁⲅⲁⲑⲟⲥ ⲣ̅ⲣⲱⲙⲉ
ϣⲁϥⲉⲓⲛⲉ ⲛ̅ⲟⲩⲁⲅⲁⲑⲟⲛ ⲉⲃⲟⲗ ϩⲙ̅ ⲡⲉϥⲉϩⲟ
ⲟⲩⲕⲁⲕ[ⲟⲥ] ˈ ⲣ̅ⲣⲱⲙⲉ ϣⲁϥⲉⲓⲛⲉ ⲛ̅ϩⲛ̅ⲡⲟⲛⲏⲣⲟⲛ ⲉⲃⲟⲗ
ˈ ϩⲙ̅ ⲡⲉϥⲉϩⲟ ⲉⲑⲟⲟⲩ ⲉⲧϩⲛ̅ ⲡⲉϥϩⲏⲧ ⲁⲩⲱ ⲛ̅ϥϫⲱ
ⲛ̅ϩⲛ̅ⲡⲟⲛⲏⲣⲟⲛ ⲉⲃⲟⲗ ⲅⲁⲣ ϩⲙ̅ [5] ⲫⲟⲩⲟ ⲙ̅ⲫⲏⲧ
ϣⲁϥⲉⲓⲛⲉ ⲉⲃⲟⲗ ⲛ̅ϩⲛ̅ⲡⲟˈⲛⲏⲣⲟⲛ

46   ⲡⲉϫⲉ ⲓ̅ⲥ̅ ϫⲉ ϫⲓⲛ ⲁⲇⲁⲙ ϣⲁ ⲓ̈ⲱϩⲁⲛˈⲛⲏⲥ
ⲡⲃⲁⲡⲧⲓⲥⲧⲏⲥ ϩⲛ̅ ⲛ̅ϫⲡⲟ ⲛ̅ⲛϩⲓⲟⲙⲉ ˈ ⲙ̅ⲛ̅ ⲡⲉⲧϫⲟⲥⲉ
ⲁⲓ̈ⲱϩⲁⲛⲛⲏⲥ ⲡⲃⲁⲡⲧⲓˈⲥⲧⲏⲥ ϣⲓⲛⲁ ϫⲉ ⲛⲟⲩⲱϭⲡ
ⲛ̅ϭⲓ ⲛⲉϥⲃⲁⲗ [10] ⲁⲉⲓϫⲟⲟⲥ ⲇⲉ ϫⲉ ⲡⲉⲧⲛⲁϣⲱⲡⲉ ϩⲛ̅
ⲧⲏⲩⲧⲛ̅ ⲉϥⲟ ⲛ̅ⲕⲟⲩⲉⲓ ϥⲛⲁⲥⲟⲩⲱⲛ ⲧⲙ̅ⲛ̅ⲧⲉˈⲣⲟ ⲁⲩⲱ
ϥⲛⲁϫⲓⲥⲉ ⲁⲓ̈ⲱϩⲁⲛⲛⲏⲥ

42   Jesus said, "Be passersby."

43   His followers said to him, "Who are you to say these things to us?"

"You do not know who I am from what I say to you. Rather, you have become like the Jewish people, for they love the tree but hate its fruit, or they love the fruit but hate the tree."

44   Jesus said, "Whoever blasphemes against the father will be forgiven, and whoever blasphemes against the son will be forgiven, but whoever blasphemes against the holy spirit will not be forgiven, either on earth or in heaven."

45   Jesus said, "Grapes are not harvested from thorn trees, nor are figs gathered from thistles, for they yield no fruit. A good person brings forth good from the storehouse; a bad person brings forth evil things from the corrupt storehouse in the heart and says evil things. For from the abundance of the heart this person brings forth evil things."

46   Jesus said, "From Adam to John the Baptist, among those born of women, no one is so much greater than John the Baptist that the person's eyes should not be averted. But I have said that whoever among you becomes a child will know the kingdom and will become greater than John."

47 ⲡⲉϫⲉ ⲓ̅ⲥ̅ ϫⲉ ⲙⲛ̅ ϭⲟⲙ ⲛ̅ⲧⲉⲟⲩⲣⲱⲙⲉ ⲧⲉⲗⲟ ⲁϩⲧⲟ
ⲥⲛⲁⲩ ⲛ̅ϥϫⲱⲗⲕ ⲙ̅ⲡⲓⲧⲉ ⲥⲛ̅ⲧⲉ ⲁⲩⲱ ⲙⲛ̅ [15] ϭⲟⲙ
ⲛ̅ⲧⲉⲟⲩϩⲙ̅ϩⲁⲗ ϣⲙ̅ϣⲉ ϫⲟⲉⲓⲥ ⲥⲛⲁⲩ ⲏ ϥⲛⲁⲣ̅ⲧⲓⲙⲁ
ⲙ̅ⲡⲟⲩⲁ ⲁⲩⲱ ⲡⲕⲉⲟⲩⲁ ϥⲛⲁⲣ̅ϩⲩⲃⲣⲓⲍⲉ ⲙ̅ⲙⲟϥ
ⲙⲁⲣⲉⲣⲱⲙⲉ ⲥⲉ ⲣ̅ⲡⲁⲥ ⲁⲩⲱ ⲛ̅ⲧⲉⲩⲛⲟⲩ
ⲛ̅ϥⲉⲡⲓⲑⲩⲙⲉⲓ ⲁⲥⲱ ⲏⲣⲡ ⲃ̅ⲃⲣ̅ⲣⲉ ⲁⲩⲱ ⲙⲁⲩⲛⲟⲩϫ
ⲏⲣⲡ ⲃ̅ⲃⲣ̅ⲣⲉ ⲉⲁⲥ[20]ⲕⲟⲥ ⲛ̅ⲁⲥ ϫⲉⲕⲁⲁⲥ ⲛ̅ⲛⲟⲩⲡⲱϩ
ⲁⲩⲱ ⲙⲁⲩⲛⲉϫ ⲏⲣⲡ ⲛ̅ⲁⲥ ⲉⲁⲥⲕⲟⲥ ⲃ̅ⲃⲣ̅ⲣⲉ ϣⲓⲛⲁ
ϫⲉ ⲛⲉϥⲧⲉⲕⲁϥ ⲙⲁⲧϫⲁⲅ ⲧⲟⲉⲓⲥ ⲛ̅ⲁⲥ ⲁϣⲧⲏⲛ
ⲛ̅ϣⲁⲉⲓ ⲉⲡⲉⲓ ⲟⲩⲛ ⲟⲩⲡⲱϩ ⲛⲁϣⲱⲡⲉ

48 ⲡⲉϫⲉ ⲓ̅ⲥ̅ ϫⲉ ⲉⲣϣⲁⲥⲛⲁⲩ ⲣ̅ ⲉⲓⲣⲏⲛⲏ ⲙⲛ̅ [25]
ⲛⲟⲩⲉⲣⲏⲩ ϩⲙ̅ ⲡⲉⲓⲏⲉⲓ ⲟⲩⲱⲧ ⲥⲉⲛⲁϫⲟⲟⲥ ⲙ̅ⲡⲧⲁⲩ
ϫⲉ ⲡⲱⲛⲉ ⲉⲃⲟⲗ ⲁⲩⲱ ϥⲛⲁⲡⲱⲱⲛⲉ

49 ⲡⲉϫⲉ ⲓ̅ⲥ̅ ϫⲉ ϩⲉⲛⲙⲁⲕⲁⲣⲓⲟⲥ ⲛⲉ ⲛⲓⲙⲟⲛⲁⲭⲟⲥ
ⲁⲩⲱ ⲉⲧⲥⲟⲧⲡ ϫⲉ ⲧⲉⲧⲛⲁϩⲉ ⲁⲧⲙ̅ⲛ̅ⲧⲉⲣⲟ ϫⲉ
ⲛ̅ⲧⲱⲧⲛ̅ ϩⲛ̅ⲉⲃⲟⲗ [30] ⲛ̅ϩⲏⲧⲥ̅ ⲡⲁⲗⲓⲛ ⲉⲧⲉⲧⲛⲁⲃⲱⲕ
ⲉⲙⲁⲩ

50 ⲡⲉϫⲉ ⲓ̅ⲥ̅ ϫⲉ ⲉⲩϣⲁⲛϫⲟⲟⲥ ⲛⲏⲧⲛ̅ ϫⲉ
ⲛ̅ⲧⲁⲧⲉⲧⲛ̅ϣⲱⲡⲉ ⲉⲃⲟⲗ ⲧⲱⲛ ϫⲟⲟⲥ ⲛⲁⲩ ϫⲉ
ⲛ̅ⲧⲁⲛⲉⲓ ⲉⲃⲟⲗ ϩⲙ̅ ⲡⲟⲩⲟⲉⲓⲛ ⲡⲙⲁ ⲉⲛⲧⲁⲡⲟⲩⲟⲉⲓⲛ
ϣⲱⲡⲉ ⲙ̅ⲙⲁⲩ ⲉⲃⲟⲗ [35] ϩⲓⲧⲟⲟⲧϥ ⲟⲩⲁⲁⲧϥ ⲁϥⲱϩⲉ
ⲉⲣⲁⲧϥ] 42 ⲁⲩⲱ ⲁϥⲟⲩⲱⲛϩ ⲉ[ⲃ]ⲟⲗ ϩⲛ̅ ⲧⲟⲩϩⲓⲕⲱⲛ
ⲉⲩϣⲁϫⲟⲟⲥ ⲛⲏⲧⲛ̅ ϫⲉ ⲛ̅ⲧⲱⲧⲛ̅ ⲡⲉ ϫⲟⲟⲥ ϫⲉ
ⲁⲛⲟⲛ ⲛⲉϥϣⲏⲣⲉ ⲁⲩⲱ ⲁⲛⲟⲛ ⲛ̅ⲥⲱⲧⲡ ⲙ̅ⲡⲉⲓⲱⲧ
ⲉⲧⲟⲛϩ ⲉⲩϣⲁⲛϫⲛⲉ ⲧⲏⲩⲧⲛ̅ [5] ϫⲉ ⲟⲩ ⲡⲉ ⲡⲙⲁⲉⲓⲛ
ⲙ̅ⲡⲉⲧⲛ̅ⲉⲓⲱⲧ ⲉⲧϩⲛ̅ ⲧⲏⲩⲧⲛ̅ ϫⲟⲟⲥ ⲉⲣⲟⲟⲩ ϫⲉ
ⲟⲩⲕⲓⲙ ⲡⲉ ⲙⲛ̅ ⲟⲩⲁⲛⲁⲡⲁⲩⲥⲓⲥ

51 ⲡⲉϫⲁⲩ ⲛⲁϥ ⲛ̅ϭⲓ ⲛⲉϥⲙⲁⲑⲏⲧⲏⲥ ϫⲉ ⲁϣ
ⲛ̅ϩⲟⲟⲩ ⲉⲧⲁⲛⲁⲡⲁⲩⲥⲓⲥ ⲛ̅ⲛⲉⲧⲙⲟⲟⲩⲧ ⲛⲁϣⲱⲡⲉ
ⲁⲩⲱ ⲁϣ ⲛ̅ϩⲟⲟⲩ [10] ⲉⲡⲕⲟⲥⲙⲟⲥ ⲃ̅ⲃⲣ̅ⲣⲉ ⲛⲏⲩ
ⲡⲉϫⲁϥ ⲛⲁⲩ ϫⲉ ⲧⲏ ⲉⲧⲉⲧⲛ̅ϭⲱϣⲧ ⲉⲃⲟⲗ ϩⲏⲧⲥ̅
ⲁⲥⲉⲓ ⲁⲗⲗⲁ ⲛ̅ⲧⲱⲧⲛ̅ ⲧⲉⲧⲛ̅ⲥⲟⲟⲩⲛ ⲁⲛ ⲙ̅ⲙⲟⲥ

47   Jesus said, "A person cannot mount two horses or bend two bows. And a servant cannot serve two masters, or that servant will honor the one and offend the other. No person drinks aged wine and immediately desires to drink new wine. New wine is not poured into aged wineskins, or they might break, and aged wine is not poured into a new wineskin, or it might spoil. An old patch is not sewn onto a new garment, for there would be a tear."

48   Jesus said, "If two make peace with each other in a single house, they will say to the mountain, 'Move from here,' and it will move."

49   Jesus said, "Fortunate are those who are alone and chosen, for you will find the kingdom. For you have come from it, and you will return there again."

50   Jesus said, "If they say to you, 'Where have you come from?' say to them, 'We have come from the light, from the place where the light came into being by itself, established [itself], and appeared in their image.' If they say to you, 'Is it you?' say, 'We are its children, and we are the chosen of the living father.' If they ask you, 'What is the evidence of your father in you?' say to them, 'It is motion and rest.' "

51   His followers said to him, "When will the rest for the dead take place, and when will the new world come?"

He said to them, "What you look for has come, but you do not know it."

52   пеϫⲁⲩ ' naϥ ⲛ̄ϭⲓ ⲛⲉϥⲙⲁⲑⲏⲧⲏⲥ ϫⲉ
ϫⲟⲩⲧⲁϥⲧⲉ ' ⲙ̄ⲡⲣⲟⲫⲏⲧⲏⲥ ⲁⲩϣⲁϫⲉ ϩⲙ̄ ⲡⲓⲥⲣⲁⲏⲗ
[15] ⲁⲩⲱ ⲁⲩϣⲁϫⲉ ⲧⲏⲣⲟⲩ ϩⲣⲁⲓ̈ ⲛ̄ϩⲏⲧⲕ
      ⲡⲉϫⲁϥ ⲛⲁⲩ ϫⲉ ⲁⲧⲉⲧⲛ̄ⲕⲱ ⲙ̄ⲡⲉⲧⲟⲛϩ
ⲙ̄ⲡⲉⲧⲛ̄ⲙ̄ⲧⲟ ⲉⲃⲟⲗ ⲁⲩⲱ ⲁⲧⲉⲧⲛ̄ϣⲁϫⲉ ϩⲁ
ⲛⲉⲧ'ⲙⲟⲟⲩⲧ

53   ⲡⲉϫⲁⲩ ⲛⲁⲩ ⲛ̄ϭⲓ ⲛⲉϥⲙⲁⲑⲏⲧⲏⲥ ' ϫⲉ ⲡⲥⲃ̄ⲃⲉ
ⲣ̄ⲱⲫⲉⲗⲉⲓ ⲏ ⲙ̄ⲙⲟⲛ
      ⲡⲉϫⲁϥ [20] ⲛⲁⲩ ϫⲉ ⲛⲉⲩⲣ̄ⲱⲫⲉⲗⲉⲓ ⲛⲉⲡⲟⲩⲉⲓⲱⲧ
ⲛⲁ'ϫⲡⲟⲟⲩ ⲉⲃⲟⲗ ϩⲛ̄ ⲧⲟⲩⲙⲁⲁⲩ ⲉⲩⲥⲃ̄ⲃⲏⲩ ' ⲁⲗⲗⲁ
ⲡⲥⲃ̄ⲃⲉ ⲙ̄ⲙⲉ ϩⲙ̄ ⲡⲛ̄ⲁ ⲁϥϭⲛ̄ ϩⲏⲩ ' ⲧⲏⲣϥ

54   ⲡⲉϫⲉ ⲓ̄ⲥ̄ ϫⲉ ϩⲛ̄ⲙⲁⲕⲁⲣⲓⲟⲥ ⲛⲉ ⲛϩⲏ'ⲕⲉ ϫⲉ
ⲧⲱⲧⲛ̄ ⲧⲉ ⲧⲙ̄ⲛ̄ⲧⲉⲣⲟ ⲛ̄ⲙ̄ⲡⲏⲩⲉ [25]

55   ⲡⲉϫⲉ ⲓ̄ⲥ̄ ϫⲉ ⲡⲉⲧⲁⲙⲉⲥⲧⲉ ⲡⲉϥⲉⲓⲱⲧ ' ⲁⲛ ⲙⲛ̄
ⲧⲉϥⲙⲁⲁⲩ ϥⲛⲁϣⲣ̄ ⲙⲁⲑⲏⲧⲏⲥ ⲁⲛ ' ⲛⲁⲉⲓ ⲁⲩⲱ
ⲛ̄ϥⲙⲉⲥⲧⲉ ⲛⲉϥⲥⲛⲏⲩ ⲙⲛ̄ ' ⲛⲉϥⲥⲱⲛⲉ ⲛ̄ϥϥⲓ
ⲙ̄ⲡⲉϥⲥⲣⲟⲥ ⲛ̄ⲧⲁϩⲉ ' ϥⲛⲁϣⲱⲡⲉ ⲁⲛ ⲉϥⲟ ⲛ̄ⲁϯ̄ⲟⲥ
ⲛⲁⲉⲓ

56   ⲡⲉ[30]ϫⲉ ⲓ̄ⲥ̄ ϫⲉ ⲡⲉⲧⲁϩⲥⲟⲩⲱⲛ ⲡⲕⲟⲥⲙⲟⲥ ⲁϥϩⲉ
ⲉⲩⲡⲧⲱⲙⲁ ⲁⲩⲱ ⲡⲉⲛⲧⲁϩϩⲉⲉ ⲁⲡⲧⲱⲙⲁ ⲡⲕⲟⲥⲙⲟⲥ
ⲙ̄ⲡϣⲁ ⲙ̄ⲙⲟϥ ⲁⲛ

57   ⲡⲉϫⲉ ⲓ̄ⲥ̄ ϫⲉ ⲧⲙ̄ⲛ̄ⲧⲉⲣⲟ ⲙ̄ⲡⲉⲓⲱⲧ ⲉⲥⲛ̄ⲧⲱⲛ '
ⲁⲩⲣⲱⲙⲉ ⲉⲩⲛ̄ⲧⲁϥ ⲙ̄ⲙⲁⲩ ⲛ̄ⲛⲟⲩϭⲣⲟϭ [35] ⲉⲛ̣[ⲁⲛⲟ]ⲩϥ
ⲁⲡⲉϥϫⲁϫⲉ ⲉⲓ ⲛ̄ⲧⲟⲩϣⲏ 43 ⲁϥⲥⲓⲧⲉ
ⲛ̄ⲟⲩϫⲓϫⲁⲛⲓ[ⲟ]ⲛ ⲉϫ̄ⲛ̄ ⲡⲉϭⲣⲟ[ϭ ⲉ]'ⲧⲛⲁⲛⲟⲩϥ
ⲙ̄ⲡⲉⲡⲣⲱⲙⲉ ⲕⲟⲟⲩ ⲉϩⲱⲗⲉ ' ⲙ̄ⲡϫⲓϫⲁⲛⲓⲟⲛ ⲡⲉϫⲁϥ
ⲛⲁⲩ ϫⲉ ⲙⲏⲡⲱⲥ ' ⲛ̄ⲧⲉⲧⲛ̄ⲃⲱⲕ ϫⲉ ⲉⲛⲁϩⲱⲗⲉ
ⲙ̄ⲡϫⲓϫⲁⲛⲓⲟⲛ [5] ⲛ̄ⲧⲉⲧⲛ̄ϩⲱⲗⲉ ⲙ̄ⲡⲥⲟⲩⲟ ⲛⲙ̄ⲙⲁϥ ϩⲙ̄
ⲫⲟ'ⲟⲩ ⲅⲁⲣ ⲙ̄ⲡⲱϩⲥ̄ ⲛ̄ϫⲓϫⲁⲛⲓⲟⲛ ⲛⲁⲟⲩⲱⲛϩ ' ⲉⲃⲟⲗ
ⲥⲉϩⲟⲗⲟⲩ ⲛ̄ⲥⲉⲣⲟⲕϩⲟⲩ

58   ⲡⲉϫⲉ ⲓ̄ⲥ̄ ' ϫⲉ ⲟⲩⲙⲁⲕⲁⲣⲓⲟⲥ ⲡⲉ ⲡⲣⲱⲙⲉ
ⲛ̄ⲧⲁϩϩⲓⲥⲉ ' ⲁϥϩⲉ ⲁⲡⲱⲛϩ

52   His followers said to him, "Twenty-four prophets have spoken in Israel, and they all spoke of you."

He said to them, "You have disregarded the living one who is in your presence and have spoken of the dead."

53   His followers said to him, "Is circumcision useful or not?"

He said to them, "If it were useful, children's fathers would produce them already circumcised from their mothers. Rather, the true circumcision in spirit has become valuable in every respect."

54   Jesus said, "Fortunate are the poor, for yours is heaven's kingdom."

55   Jesus said, "Whoever does not hate father and mother cannot be a follower of me, and whoever does not hate brothers and sisters and bear the cross as I do will not be worthy of me."

56   Jesus said, "Whoever has come to know the world has discovered a carcass, and whoever has discovered a carcass, of that person the world is not worthy."

57   Jesus said, "The father's kingdom is like a person who had [good] seed. His enemy came at night and sowed weeds among the good seed. The person did not let them pull up the weeds, but said to them, 'No, or you might go to pull up the weeds and pull up the wheat along with them.' For on the day of the harvest the weeds will be conspicuous and will be pulled up and burned."

58   Jesus said, "Fortunate is the person who has worked hard and has found life."

59 пєжє ⲓ̅ⲥ̅ жє ϭⲱϣⲧ ⲛ̅ⲥⲁ ⲡⲉ[10]ⲧⲟⲛϩ ϩⲱⲥ
ⲉⲧⲉⲧⲛ̅ⲟⲛϩ ϩⲓⲛⲁ жє ⲛⲉⲧⲙ̅ⲙⲟⲩ ' ⲁⲩⲱ ⲛ̅ⲧⲉⲧⲛ̅ϣⲓⲛⲉ
ⲉⲛⲁⲩ ⲉⲣⲟⲩ ⲁⲩⲱ ⲧⲉⲧⲛⲁϣϭ̅ⲙ̅ ϭⲟⲙ ⲁⲛ ⲉⲛⲁⲩ

60 ‹ⲁⲩⲛⲁⲩ› ⲁⲩⲥⲁⲙⲁⲣⲉⲓⲧⲏⲥ ⲉⲩϥⲓ ⲛ̅ⲛⲟⲩϩⲓⲉⲓⲃ
ⲉⲩⲃⲏⲕ ⲉϩⲟⲩⲛ ⲉⲧⲟⲩⲇⲁⲓⲁ

ⲡⲉ'жⲁⲩ ⲛ̅ⲛⲉⲩⲙⲁⲑⲏⲧⲏⲥ жє ⲡⲏ ⲙ̅ⲡⲕⲱⲧⲉ [15]
ⲙ̅ⲡⲉϩⲓⲉⲓⲃ

ⲡⲉжⲁⲩ ⲛⲁⲩ жⲉⲕⲁⲁⲥ ⲉⲩⲛⲁ'ⲙⲟⲟⲩⲧϥ
ⲛ̅ϥⲟⲩⲟⲙϥ

ⲡⲉжⲁⲩ ⲛⲁⲩ ϩⲱⲥ ⲉ'ϥⲟⲛϩ ϥⲛⲁⲟⲩⲟⲙϥ ⲁⲛ
ⲁⲗⲗⲁ ⲉⲩϣⲁⲙⲟ'ⲟⲩⲧϥ ⲛ̅ϥϣⲱⲡⲉ ⲛ̅ⲟⲩⲡⲧⲱⲙⲁ

ⲡⲉжⲁⲩ ' жⲉ ⲛ̅ⲕⲉⲥⲙⲟⲧ ϥⲛⲁϣⲁⲥ ⲁⲛ

ⲡⲉжⲁⲩ ⲛⲁⲩ [20] жⲉ ⲛ̅ⲧⲱⲧⲛ̅ ϩⲱⲧⲧⲏⲩⲧⲛ̅ ϣⲓⲛⲉ
ⲛ̅ⲥⲁ ⲟⲩ'ⲧⲟⲡⲟⲥ ⲛⲏⲧⲛ̅ ⲉϩⲟⲩⲛ ⲉⲧⲁⲛⲁⲡⲁⲩⲥⲓⲥ '
жⲉⲕⲁⲁⲥ ⲛ̅ⲛⲉⲧⲛ̅ϣⲱⲡⲉ ⲙ̅ⲡⲧⲱⲙⲁ ⲛ̅ⲥⲉ'ⲟⲩⲱⲙ
ⲧⲏⲩⲧⲛ̅

61 ⲡⲉжⲉ ⲓ̅ⲥ̅ ⲟⲩⲛ̅ ⲥⲛⲁⲩ ⲛⲁⲙ̅ⲧⲟⲛ ⲙ̅ⲙⲁⲩ ϩⲓ
ⲟⲩϭⲗⲟϭ ⲡⲟⲩⲁ ⲛⲁⲙⲟⲩ ⲡⲟⲩ[25]ⲁ ⲛⲁⲱⲛϩ

ⲡⲉжⲉ ⲥⲁⲗⲱⲙⲏ ⲛ̅ⲧⲁⲕ ⲛⲓⲙ ' ⲡⲣⲱⲙⲉ ϩⲱⲥ ⲉⲃⲟⲗ
ϩⲛ̅ ⲟⲩⲁ ⲁⲕⲧⲉⲗⲟ ⲉжⲙ̅ ' ⲡⲁϭⲗⲟϭ ⲁⲩⲱ ⲁⲕⲟⲩⲱⲙ
ⲉⲃⲟⲗ ϩⲛ̅ ⲧⲁ'ⲧⲣⲁⲡⲉⲍⲁ

ⲡⲉжⲉ ⲓ̅ⲥ̅ ⲛⲁⲥ жⲉ ⲁⲛⲟⲕ ⲡⲉ ' ⲡⲉⲧϣⲟⲟⲡ ⲉⲃⲟⲗ
ϩⲙ̅ ⲡⲉⲧϣⲏϣ ⲁⲩϯ [30] ⲛⲁⲉⲓ ⲉⲃⲟⲗ ϩⲛ̅ ⲛⲁ ⲡⲁⲉⲓⲱⲧ
ⲁⲛⲟⲕ ⲧⲉⲕ'ⲙⲁⲑⲏⲧⲏⲥ

ⲉⲧⲃⲉ ⲡⲁⲉⲓ ϯжⲱ ⲙ̅ⲙⲟⲥ жⲉ ' ϩⲟⲧⲁⲛ ⲉϥϣⲁϣⲱⲡⲉ
ⲉϥϣⲏ‹ϣ› ϥⲛⲁⲙⲟⲩϩ ' ⲟⲩⲟⲉⲓⲛ ϩⲟⲧⲁⲛ ⲇⲉ
ⲉϥϣⲁⲛϣⲱⲡⲉ ⲉϥⲡⲏϣ ϥⲛⲁⲙⲟⲩϩ ⲛ̅ⲕⲁⲕⲉ

62 ⲡⲉжⲉ ⲓ̅ⲥ̅ жⲉ ⲉⲓ̈[35]жⲱ ⲛ̅ⲛⲁⲙⲩⲥⲧⲏⲣⲓⲟⲛ
ⲛ̅ⲛⲉ[ⲧⲙ̅ⲡϣⲁ] ⲛ̅44[ⲛⲁ]ⲙⲩⲥⲧⲏⲣⲓⲟⲛ ⲡⲉ[ⲧ]ⲉ
ⲧⲉⲕⲟⲩⲛⲁⲙ ⲛⲁⲁϥ ' ⲙ̅ⲡⲧⲣⲉⲧⲉⲕϩⲃⲟⲩⲣ ⲉⲓⲙⲉ жⲉ ⲉⲥⲣ
ⲟⲩ

59   Jesus said, "Look to the living one as long as you live, or you might die and then try to see the living one, and you will be unable to see."

60   <He saw> a Samaritan carrying a lamb as he was going to Judea.

He said to his followers, "<. . .> that person <. . .> around the lamb."

They said to him, "So that he may kill it and eat it."

He said to them, "He will not eat it while it is alive, but only after he has killed it and it has become a carcass."

They said, "Otherwise he cannot do it."

He said to them, "So also with you, seek for yourselves a place for rest, or you might become a carcass and be eaten."

61   Jesus said, "Two will rest on a couch; one will die, one will live."

Salome said, "Who are you, mister? You have climbed onto my couch and eaten from my table as if you are from someone."

Jesus said to her, "I am the one who comes from what is whole. I was given from the things of my father."

"I am your follower."

"For this reason I say, if one is <whole>, one will be filled with light, but if one is divided, one will be filled with darkness."

62   Jesus said, "I disclose my mysteries to those [who are worthy] of [my] mysteries. Do not let your left hand know what your right hand is doing."

63 ΠΕϪΕ I͞C Ϫε ΝΕΥN̄ ΟΥΡϢΜΕ M̄ΠλΟΥCΙΟC
ΕΥN̄ΤΑϤ M̄ΜΑΥ N̄ϩΑϩ N̄ΧΡΗΜΑ ΠΕϪΑϤ Ϫε
†ΝΑP̄ΧΡϢ N̄⁵ΝΑΧΡΗΜΑ ϪΕΚΑΑC ΕΕΙΝΑϪΟ
N̄ΤΑϢCϩ ΝΤΑΤϢϬΕ N̄ΤΑΜΟΥϩ N̄ΝΑΕϩϢΡ
N̄ΚΑΡΠΟC ϢΙΝΑ Ϫε ΝΙP̄ ϬΡϢϩ λ̄λΑΑΥ ΝΑΕΙ
ΝΕΝΕϤΜΕΕΥΕ ΕΡΟΟΥ ϩN̄ ΠΕϤϩΗΤ ΑΥϢ ϩN̄
ΤΟΥϢΗ ΕΤM̄ΜΑΥ ΑϤΜΟΥ ΠΕΤΕΥN̄ ΜΑϪΕ ¹⁰M̄ΜΟϤ
ΜΑΡΕϤCϢΤM̄

63   Jesus said, "There was a rich person who had a great deal of money. He said, 'I shall invest my money so that I may sow, reap, plant, and fill my storehouses with produce, that I may lack nothing.' These were the things he was thinking in his heart, but that very night he died. Whoever has ears should hear."

ⲡⲉϫⲉ ⲓ̄ⲥ̄ ϫⲉ ⲟⲩⲣⲱⲙⲉ ⲛⲉⲩⲛ̄ⲧⲁⲩ ⲉ̅ⲛ̄ϣⲙ̄ⲙⲟ
ⲁⲩⲱ ⲛ̄ⲧⲁⲣⲉϥⲥⲟⲃⲧⲉ ⲙ̄ⲡⲇⲓⲡⲛⲟⲛ ⲁϥϫⲟⲟⲩ
ⲙ̄ⲡⲉϥϩⲙ̄ϩⲁⲗ ϣⲓ̈ⲛⲁ ⲉϥⲛⲁⲧⲱϩⲙ̄ ⲛ̄ⲛ̄ϣⲙ̄ⲙⲟⲉⲓ

ⲁϥⲃⲱⲕ ⲙ̄ⲡϣⲟⲣⲡ ⲡⲉϫⲁϥ ⲛⲁϥ ϫⲉ ⲡⲁϫⲟⲉⲓⲥ
ⲧⲱϩⲙ̄ 15 ⲙ̄ⲙⲟⲕ

ⲡⲉϫⲁϥ ϫⲉ ⲟⲩⲛ̄ⲧⲁⲉⲓ ⲉⲛ̄ϩⲟⲙⲧ ⲁϩⲉⲛⲉⲙⲡⲟⲣⲟⲥ
ⲥⲉⲛ̄ⲛⲏⲩ ϣⲁⲣⲟⲉⲓ ⲉⲣⲟⲩϩⲉ ϯⲛⲁⲃⲱⲕ ⲛ̄ⲧⲁⲟⲩⲉϩ
ⲥⲁϩⲛⲉ ⲛⲁⲩ ϯⲣ̄ⲡⲁⲣⲁⲓⲧⲉⲓ ⲙ̄ⲡⲇⲓⲡⲛⲟⲛ

ⲁϥⲃⲱⲕ ϣⲁ ⲕⲉⲟⲩⲁ ⲡⲉϫⲁϥ ⲛⲁⲩ ϫⲉ
ⲁⲡⲁϫⲟⲉⲓⲥ ⲧⲱϩⲙ̄ ⲙ̄ⲙⲟⲕ 20

ⲡⲉϫⲁϥ ⲛⲁⲩ ϫⲉ ⲁⲉⲓⲧⲟⲟⲩ ⲟⲩⲏⲉⲓ ⲁⲩⲱ
ⲥⲉⲣⲁⲓⲧⲉⲓ ⲙ̄ⲙⲟⲉⲓ ⲛ̄ⲟⲩϩⲙⲉⲣⲁ ϯⲛⲁⲥⲣ̄ϥⲉ ⲁⲛ

ⲁϥⲉⲓ ϣⲁ ⲕⲉⲟⲩⲁ ⲡⲉϫⲁϥ ⲛⲁⲩ ϫⲉ ⲡⲁϫⲟⲉⲓⲥ
ⲧⲱϩⲙ̄ ⲙ̄ⲙⲟⲕ

ⲡⲉϫⲁϥ ⲛⲁⲩ ϫⲉ ⲡⲁϣⲃⲏⲣ ⲛⲁⲣ̄ ϣⲉⲗⲉⲉⲧ ⲁⲩⲱ
ⲁⲛⲟⲕ ⲉⲧⲛⲁⲣ̄ ϫⲓⲡⲛⲟⲛ 25 ϯⲛⲁϣⲓ ⲁⲛ ϯⲣ̄ⲡⲁⲣⲁⲓⲧⲉⲓ
ⲙ̄ⲡⲇⲓⲡⲛⲟⲛ

ⲁϥⲃⲱⲕ ϣⲁ ⲕⲉⲟⲩⲁ ⲡⲉϫⲁϥ ⲛⲁⲩ ϫⲉ ⲡⲁϫⲟⲉⲓⲥ
ⲧⲱϩⲙ̄ ⲙ̄ⲙⲟⲕ

ⲡⲉϫⲁϥ ⲛⲁⲩ ϫⲉ ⲁⲉⲓⲧⲟⲟⲩ ⲛ̄ⲟⲩⲕⲱⲙⲏ ⲉⲉⲓⲃⲏⲕ
ⲁϫⲓ ⲛ̄ϣⲱⲙ ϯⲛⲁϣⲓ ⲁⲛ ϯⲣ̄ⲡⲁⲣⲁⲓⲧⲉⲓ

ⲁϥⲉⲓ ⲛ̄ϭⲓ ⲡϩⲙ̄ϩⲁⲗ ⲁϥϫⲟ30ⲟⲥ ⲁⲡⲉϥϫⲟⲉⲓⲥ ϫⲉ
ⲛⲉⲛⲧⲁⲕⲧⲁϩⲙⲟⲩ ⲁ ⲡⲇⲓⲡⲛⲟⲛ ⲁⲩⲡⲁⲣⲁⲓⲧⲉⲓ

ⲡⲉϫⲉ ⲡϫⲟⲉⲓⲥ ⲙ̄ⲡⲉϥϩⲙ̄ϩⲁⲗ ϫⲉ ⲃⲱⲕ ⲉⲡⲥⲁ
ⲛⲃⲟⲗ ⲁⲛϩⲓⲟⲟⲩⲉ ⲛⲉⲧⲕⲛⲁϩⲉ ⲉⲣⲟⲟⲩ ⲉⲛⲓⲟⲩ
ϫⲉⲕⲁⲁⲥ ⲉⲩⲛⲁⲣ̄ϫⲓⲡⲛⲉⲓ

ⲛ̄ⲣⲉϥⲧⲟⲟⲩ ⲙ̄ⲛ̄ ⲛⲉϣⲟ35ⲧ[ⲉ ⲥⲉⲛⲁⲃ]ⲱⲕ ⲁⲛ
ⲉϩⲟⲩⲛ ⲉⲛⲧⲟⲡⲟⲥ ⲙ̄ⲡⲁⲓ̈ⲱⲧ 45

64   Jesus said, "A person was receiving guests. When he had prepared the dinner, he sent his servant to invite the guests.

"The servant went to the first and said to that one, 'My master invites you.'

"That person said, 'Some merchants owe me money; they are coming to me tonight. I must go and give them instructions. Please excuse me from dinner.'

"The servant went to another and said to that one, 'My master has invited you.'

"That person said to the servant, 'I have bought a house and I have been called away for a day. I shall have no time.'

"The servant went to another and said to that one, 'My master invites you.'

"That person said to the servant, 'My friend is to be married and I am to arrange the banquet. I shall not be able to come. Please excuse me from dinner.'

"The servant went to another and said to that one, 'My master invites you.'

"That person said to the servant, 'I have bought an estate and I am going to collect the rent. I shall not be able to come. Please excuse me.'

"The servant returned and said to his master, 'The people whom you invited to dinner have asked to be excused.'

"The master said to his servant, 'Go out on the streets and bring back whomever you find to have dinner.'

"Buyers and merchants [will] not enter the places of my father."

65   ⲡⲉϫⲁϥ ϫⲉ ⲟⲩⲣⲱⲙⲉ ⲛ̄ⲭⲣⲏ[ⲥⲧ.]ⲥ ⲛⲉⲩⲛ̄ⲧ[ⲁϥ]
ⲛ̄ⲟⲩⲙⲁ ⲛ̄ⲉⲗⲟⲟⲗⲉ ⲁϥⲧⲁⲁϥ ⲛ̄ϩⲉⲛⲟⲩⲟⲉⲓⲉ ϣⲓⲛⲁ
ⲉⲩⲛⲁⲣ̄ ϩⲱⲃ ⲉⲣⲟϥ ⲛ̄ϥϫⲓ ⲙ̄ⲡⲉϥⲕⲁⲣⲡⲟⲥ ⲛ̄ⲧⲟⲟⲧⲟⲩ
ⲁϥϫⲟⲟⲩ ⲙ̄ⲡⲉϥϩⲙ̄ϩⲁⲗ ϫⲉ⁵ⲕⲁⲁⲥ ⲉⲛⲟⲩⲟⲉⲓⲉ ⲛⲁϯ
ⲛⲁϥ ⲙ̄ⲡⲕⲁⲣⲡⲟⲥ ⲙ̄ⲡⲙⲁ ⲛ̄ⲉⲗⲟⲟⲗⲉ ⲁⲩⲉⲙⲁϩⲧⲉ
ⲙ̄ⲡⲉϥϩⲙ̄ϩⲁⲗ ⲁⲩϩⲓⲟⲩⲉ ⲉⲣⲟϥ ⲛⲉⲕⲉⲕⲟⲩⲉⲓ ⲡⲉ
ⲛ̄ⲥⲉⲙⲟⲟⲩⲧϥ ⲁⲡϩⲙ̄ϩⲁⲗ ⲃⲱⲕ ⲁϥϫⲟⲟⲥ
ⲉⲡⲉϥϫⲟⲉⲓⲥ ⲡⲉϫⲉ ⲡⲉϥϫⲟⲉⲓⲥ ϫⲉ ⲙⲉϣⲁⲕ
ⲙ̄ⲡⲉϥⲥⲟⲩⲱ¹⁰ⲛⲟⲩ ⲁϥϫⲟⲟⲩ ⲛ̄ⲕⲉϩⲙ̄ϩⲁⲗ ⲁⲛⲟⲩⲟⲉⲓⲉ
ϩⲓⲟⲩⲉ ⲉⲡⲕⲉⲟⲩⲁ ⲧⲟⲧⲉ ⲁⲡϫⲟⲉⲓⲥ ϫⲟⲟⲩ
ⲙ̄ⲡⲉϥϣⲏⲣⲉ ⲡⲉϫⲁϥ ϫⲉ ⲙⲉϣⲁⲕ ⲥⲉⲛⲁϣⲓⲡⲉ ϩⲏⲧϥ
ⲙ̄ⲡⲁϣⲏⲣⲉ ⲁⲛⲟⲩⲟⲉⲓⲉ ⲉⲧⲙ̄ⲙⲁⲩ ⲉⲡⲉⲓ ⲥⲉⲥⲟⲟⲩⲛ
ϫⲉ ⲛ̄ⲧⲟϥ ⲡⲉ ⲡⲉⲕⲗⲏⲣⲟⲛⲟⲙⲟⲥ ¹⁵ ⲙ̄ⲡⲙⲁ ⲛ̄ⲉⲗⲟⲟⲗⲉ
ⲁⲩϭⲟⲡϥ ⲁⲩⲙⲟⲟⲩⲧϥ ⲡⲉⲧⲉⲩⲙ̄ ⲙⲁⲁϫⲉ ⲙ̄ⲙⲟϥ
ⲙⲁⲣⲉϥⲥⲱⲧⲙ̄

66   ⲡⲉϫⲉ ⲓ̅ⲥ̅ ϫⲉ ⲙⲁⲧⲥⲉⲃⲟⲉⲓ ⲉⲡⲱⲛⲉ ⲡⲁⲉⲓ
ⲛ̄ⲧⲁⲩⲥⲧⲟϥ ⲉⲃⲟⲗ ⲛ̄ϭⲓ ⲛⲉⲧⲕⲱⲧ ⲛ̄ⲧⲟϥ ⲡⲉ ⲡⲱⲛⲉ
ⲛ̄ⲕⲱϩ

67   ⲡⲉϫⲉ ⲓ̅ⲥ̅ ϫⲉ ⲡⲉⲧⲥⲟⲟⲩⲛ ⲙ̄ⲡⲧⲏⲣϥ ²⁰ⲉϥⲣ̄ ϭⲣⲱϩ
ⲟⲩⲁⲁϥ ⟨ϥⲣ̄⟩ ϭⲣⲱϩ ⲙ̄ⲡⲙⲁ ⲧⲏⲣϥ

68   ⲡⲉϫⲉ ⲓ̅ⲥ̅ ϫⲉ ⲛ̄ⲧⲱⲧⲛ̄ ϩⲙ̄ⲙⲁⲕⲁⲣⲓⲟⲥ ϩⲟⲧⲁⲛ
ⲉⲩϣⲁⲛⲙⲉⲥⲧⲉ ⲧⲏⲩⲧⲛ̄ ⲛ̄ⲥⲉⲣⲇⲓⲱⲕⲉ ⲙ̄ⲙⲱⲧⲛ̄ ⲁⲩⲱ
ⲥⲉⲛⲁϩⲉ ⲁⲛ ⲉⲧⲟⲡⲟⲥ ϩⲙ̄ ⲡⲙⲁ ⲉⲛⲧⲁⲩⲇⲓⲱⲕⲉ
ⲙ̄ⲙⲱⲧⲛ̄ ϩⲣⲁⲓ̈ ⲛ̄ϩⲏⲧϥ

69   ⲡⲉ²⁵ϫⲉ ⲓ̅ⲥ̅ ϩⲙ̄ⲙⲁⲕⲁⲣⲓⲟⲥ ⲛⲉ ⲛⲁⲉⲓ ⲛ̄ⲧⲁⲩⲇⲓⲱⲕⲉ
ⲙ̄ⲙⲟⲟⲩ ϩⲣⲁⲓ̈ ϩⲙ̄ ⲡⲟⲩϩⲏⲧ ⲛⲉⲧⲙ̄ⲙⲁⲩ
ⲛⲉⲛⲧⲁϩⲥⲟⲩⲱⲛ ⲡⲉⲓⲱⲧ ϩⲛ̄ ⲟⲩⲙⲉ ϩⲙ̄ⲙⲁⲕⲁⲣⲓⲟⲥ
ⲛⲉⲧϩⲕⲁⲉⲓⲧ ϣⲓⲛⲁ ⲉⲩⲛⲁⲧⲥⲓⲟ ⲛ̄ⲑⲏ ⲙ̄ⲡⲉⲧⲟⲩⲱϣ

70   ⲡⲉϫⲉ ⲓ̅ⲥ̅ ϩⲟ³⁰ⲧⲁⲛ ⲉⲧⲉⲧⲛ̄ϣⲁϫⲡⲉ ⲡⲏ ϩⲛ̄
ⲧⲏⲩⲧⲛ̄ ⲡⲁⲓ̈ ⲉⲧⲉⲩⲛ̄ⲧⲏⲧⲛ̄ϥ ϥⲛⲁⲧⲟⲩϫⲉ ⲧⲏⲩⲧⲛ̄
ⲉϣⲱⲡⲉ ⲙⲛ̄ⲧⲏⲧⲛ̄ ⲡⲏ ϩⲛ̄ ⲧ[ⲏ]ⲩⲧⲛ̄ ⲡⲁⲉⲓ ⲉⲧⲉ
ⲙⲛ̄ⲧⲏⲧⲛ̄ϥ ϩⲛ̄ ⲧⲏⲛⲉ ϥ[ⲛⲁ]ⲙⲟⲩⲧ ⲧⲏⲛⲉ

65   He said, "A [. . .] person owned a vineyard and rented it to some farmers, so that they might work it and he might collect its produce from them. He sent his servant so that the farmers might give the servant the produce of the vineyard. They seized, beat, and almost killed his servant, and the servant returned and told his master. His master said, 'Perhaps he did not know them.' He sent another servant, and the farmers beat that one as well. Then the master sent his son and said, 'Perhaps they will show my son some respect.' Since the farmers knew that he was the heir to the vineyard, they seized him and killed him. Whoever has ears should hear."

66   Jesus said, "Show me the stone that the builders rejected: That is the cornerstone."

67   Jesus said, "One who knows all but is lacking in oneself is utterly lacking."

68   Jesus said, "Fortunate are you when you are hated and persecuted; and no place will be found, wherever you have been persecuted."

69   Jesus said, "Fortunate are those who have been persecuted in their hearts: They are the ones who have truly come to know the father. Fortunate are they who are hungry, that the stomach of the person in want may be filled."

70   Jesus said, "If you bring forth what is within you, what you have will save you. If you do not have that within you, what you do not have within you [will] kill you."

71 πεⲍⲉ ⲓ̅ⲥ̅ ⲍⲉ ϯⲛⲁϣⲟⲣ[ϣ̅ⲣ̅ ⲙ̅ⲡⲉⲉ]ⲏⲉⲓ ³⁵ ⲁⲩⲱ
ⲙ̅ⲛ̅ ⲗⲁⲁⲩ ⲛⲁϣⲕⲟⲧϥ .[. . . . . . .] 46

72 [ⲡⲉ]ⲍ̣ⲉ̣ ⲟⲩⲣ[ⲱⲙ]ⲉ̣ ⲛⲁϥ ⲍⲉ ⲍⲟⲟⲥ ⲛ̅ⲛⲁⲥⲛⲏⲩ '
ϣⲓⲛⲁ ⲉⲩⲛⲁⲡⲱϣⲉ ⲛ̅ⲛ̅ϩⲛⲁⲁⲩ ⲙ̅ⲡⲁⲉⲓⲱⲧ ' ⲛⲙ̅ⲙⲁⲉⲓ
ⲡⲉⲍⲁϥ ⲛⲁϥ ⲍⲉ ⲱ ⲡⲣⲱⲙⲉ ⲛⲓⲙ ' ⲡⲉ ⲛ̅ⲧⲁϩⲁⲁⲧ
ⲛ̅ⲣⲉϥⲡⲱϣⲉ
ⲁϥⲕⲟⲧϥ̅ ⲁⁿⲛⲉϥⲙⲁⲑⲏⲧⲏⲥ ⲡⲉⲍⲁϥ ⲛⲁⲩ ⲍⲉ ⲙⲏ
ⲉⲉⲓϣⲟⲟⲡ ⲛ̅ⲣⲉϥⲡⲱϣⲉ

73 ⲡⲉⲍⲉ ⲓ̅ⲥ̅ ⲍⲉ ⲡⲱϩⲥ ' ⲙⲉⲛ ⲛⲁϣⲱϥ ⲛ̅ⲉⲣⲅⲁⲧⲏⲥ
ⲍⲉ ⲥⲟⲃⲕ ⲥⲟⲡⲥ̅ ' ⲍⲉ ⲙ̅ⲡⲍⲟⲉⲓⲥ ϣⲓⲛⲁ ⲉϥⲛⲁⲛⲉⲍ
ⲉⲣⲅⲁⲧⲏⲥ ' ⲉⲃⲟⲗ ⲉⲡⲱϩⲥ̅

74 ⲡⲉⲍⲁϥ ⲍⲉ ⲡⲍⲟⲉⲓⲥ ⲟⲩⲛ̅ ¹⁰ ϩⲁϩ ⲙ̅ⲡⲕⲱⲧⲉ
ⲛ̅ⲧⲍⲱⲧⲉ ⲙⲛ̅ ⲗⲁⲁⲩ ⲍⲉ ϩⲛ̅ ' ⲧϣⲱ‹ⲧ›ⲉ

75 ⲡⲉⲍⲉ ⲓ̅ⲥ̅ ⲟⲩⲛ ϩⲁϩ ⲁϩⲉⲣⲁⲧⲟⲩ ' ϩⲓⲣⲙ̅ ⲡⲣⲟ
ⲁⲗⲗⲁ ⲙ̅ⲙⲟⲛⲁⲭⲟⲥ ⲛⲉⲧⲛⲁⲃⲱⲕ ' ⲉϩⲟⲩⲛ ⲉⲡⲙⲁ
ⲛ̅ϣⲉⲗⲉⲉⲧ

76 ⲡⲉⲍⲉ ⲓ̅ⲥ̅ ⲍⲉ ' ⲧⲙ̅ⲛ̅ⲧⲉⲣⲟ ⲙ̅ⲡⲉⲓⲱⲧ ⲉⲥⲛ̅ⲧⲱⲛ
ⲁⲩⲣⲱⲙⲉ ¹⁵ ⲛ̅ⲉϣⲱⲧ ⲉⲩⲛ̅ⲧⲁϥ ⲙ̅ⲙⲁⲩ
ⲛ̅ⲟⲩⲫⲟⲣⲧⲓⲟⲛ ⲉⲁϥϩⲉ ⲁⲩⲙⲁⲣⲅⲁⲣⲓⲧⲏⲥ ⲡⲉϣⲱⲧ '
ⲉⲧⲙ̅ⲙⲁⲩ ⲟⲩⲥⲁⲃⲉ ⲡⲉ ⲁϥϯ ⲡⲉϥⲫⲟⲣⲧⲓⲟⲛ ' ⲉⲃⲟⲗ
ⲁϥⲧⲟⲟⲩ ⲛⲁϥ ⲙ̅ⲡⲓⲙⲁⲣⲅⲁⲣⲓⲧⲏⲥ ' ⲟⲩⲱⲧ ⲛ̅ⲧⲱⲧⲛ̅
ϩⲱⲧⲧⲏⲩⲧⲛ̅ ϣⲓⲛⲉ ⲛ̅²⁰ⲥⲁ ⲡⲉϥⲉϩⲟ ⲉⲙⲁϥⲱⲍⲛ̅
ⲉϥⲙⲏⲛ ⲉⲃⲟⲗ ' ⲡⲙⲁ ⲉⲙⲁⲣⲉⲍⲟⲟⲗⲉⲥ ⲧϩⲛⲟ ⲉϩⲟⲩⲛ
ⲉⲙⲁⲩ ' ⲉⲟⲩⲱⲙ ⲟⲩⲇⲉ ⲙⲁⲣⲉϥϥⲛ̅ⲧ ⲧⲁⲕⲟ

77 ⲡⲉⲍⲉ ' ⲓ̅ⲥ̅ ⲍⲉ ⲁⲛⲟⲕ ⲡⲉ ⲡⲟⲩⲟⲉⲓⲛ ⲡⲁⲉⲓ
ⲉⲧϩⲓ'ⲍⲱⲟⲩ ⲧⲏⲣⲟⲩ ⲁⲛⲟⲕ ⲡⲉ ⲡⲧⲏⲣϥ
ⲛ̅ⲧⲁ²⁵ⲡⲧⲏⲣϥ ⲉⲓ ⲉⲃⲟⲗ ⲛ̅ϩⲏⲧ ⲁⲩⲱ ⲛ̅ⲧⲁⲡⲧⲏⲣϥ '
ⲡⲱϩ ϣⲁⲣⲟⲉⲓ ⲡⲱϩ ⲛ̅ⲛⲟⲩϣⲉ ⲁⲛⲟⲕ ' ϯⲙ̅ⲙⲁⲩ ϥⲓ
ⲙ̅ⲡⲱⲛⲉ ⲉϩⲣⲁ·ⲓ ⲁⲩⲱ ⲧⲉⲧⲛⲁϩⲉ ⲉⲣⲟⲉⲓ ⲙ̅ⲙⲁⲩ

78 ⲡⲉⲍⲉ ⲓ̅ⲥ̅ ⲍⲉ ⲉⲧⲃⲉ ⲟⲩ ' ⲁⲧⲉⲧⲛ̅ⲉⲓ ⲉⲃⲟⲗ ⲉⲧⲥⲱϣⲉ
ⲉⲛⲁⲩ ⲉⲩⲕⲁϣ ³⁰ ⲉϥⲕⲓⲙ ⲉ[ⲃⲟⲗ] ϩⲓⲧⲙ̅ ⲡⲧⲏⲩ ⲁⲩⲱ
ⲉⲛⲁⲩ ' ⲉⲩⲣⲱⲙ[ⲉ ⲉ]ⲩⲛ̅ϣⲧⲏⲛ ⲉⲩϩⲏⲛ ϩⲓⲱⲱⲃ ' ⲛ̅[ⲑⲉ
ⲛ̅ⲛⲉⲧ]ⲛ̅ⲣⲣⲱⲟⲩ ⲙⲛ̅ ⲛⲉⲧⲙ̅ⲙⲉⲅⲓ₄₇ⲥⲧⲁⲛⲟⲥ ⲛⲁⲉⲓ
ⲉⲛ[ⲉ]ϣⲧⲏⲛ ⲉ[ⲧ]ϩⲏⲛ ϩⲓⲱⲟⲩ ⲁⲩⲱ ⲥⲉⲛ[ⲁ]ϣⲥ̅ⲥⲟⲩⲛ '
ⲧⲙⲉ ⲁⲛ

71   Jesus said, "I shall destroy [this] house, and no one will be able to build it [. . .]."

72   A [person said] to him, "Tell my brothers to divide my father's possessions with me."

He said to the person, "Mister, who made me a divider?"

He turned to his followers and said to them, "I am not a divider, am I?"

73   Jesus said, "The harvest is large but the workers are few. So beg the master to send out workers to the harvest."

74   He said, "Master, there are many around the drinking trough, but there is nothing in the well."

75   Jesus said, "There are many standing at the door, but those who are alone will enter the wedding chamber."

76   Jesus said, "The father's kingdom is like a merchant who had a supply of merchandise and then found a pearl. That merchant was prudent; he sold the merchandise and bought the single pearl for himself. So also with you, seek his treasure that is unfailing, that is enduring, where no moth comes to devour and no worm destroys."

77   Jesus said, "I am the light that is over all things. I am all: From me all has come forth, and to me all has reached. Split a piece of wood; I am there. Lift up the stone, and you will find me there."

78   Jesus said, "Why have you come out to the countryside? To see a reed shaken by the wind? And to see a person dressed in soft clothes, [like your] rulers and your powerful ones? They are dressed in soft clothes, and they cannot understand truth."

79 ΠΕϪΕ ΟΥⳤϨΙⲙ[Ε] ΝΑϤ ϨⲘ ΄ΠⲘΗϢΕ ϪΕ ΝΕΕΙΑΤⳉ
[Ⲛ]ΘΗ Ⲛ⁵ΤΑϨϤΙ ϨΑΡΟΚ ΑΥⲱ ⲚΚΙ[Β]Ε
ΕΝΤΑϨ΄ⳤΑΝΟΥϢΚ

ΠΕϪΑϤ ΝΑ[ⳤ] ϪΕ ΝΕ΄ΕΙΑΤΟΥ ⲚΝΕΝΤΑϨⳤⲰΤⲘ
Α΄ΠⲖΟⳤΟⳤ ⲘΠΕΙⲰΤ ΑΥΑΡΕϨ ΕΡΟϤ ΄ϨⲚ ΟΥⲙΕ ΟΥⲚ
ϨⲚϨΟΟΥ ⳌΑΡ ΝΑϢⲰΠΕ ¹⁰ ⲚΤΕΤⲚϪΟΟⳤ ϪΕ
ΝΕΕΙΑΤⳤ ⲚΘΗ ΤΑ΄ΕΙ ΕΤΕ ⲘΠⳤⲰ ΑΥⲱ ⲚΚΙΒΕ
ΝΑΕΙ ΕⲘΠΟΥ΄Ϯ ΕΡⲰΤΕ

80 ΠΕϪΕ Ιⳤ ϪΕ ΠΕΝΤΑϨⳤΟΥⲰΝ ΄ΠΚΟⳤⲙΟⳤ ΑϤϨΕ
ΕΠⳤⲰⲙΑ ΠΕΝΤΑϨϨΕ ΄ϪΕ ΕΠⳤⲰⲙΑ ΠΚΟⳤⲙΟⳤ
ⲘΠϢΑ ⲘⲙΟϤ ¹⁵ ΑΝ

81 ΠΕϪΕ Ιⳤ ϪΕ ΠΕΝΤΑϨⲢ ⲢⲘⲙΑΟ ⲙΑ΄ΡΕϤⲢ ⲢΡΟ
ΑΥⲱ ΠΕΤΕⲚΤΑϤ ⲚΟΥϪΥΝΑⲙΙⳤ ⲙΑΡΕϤΑΡΝΑ

82 ΠΕϪΕ Ιⳤ ϪΕ ΠΕΤϨΗΝ ΄ΕΡΟΕΙ ΕϤϨΗΝ ΕΤⳤΑΤΕ
ΑΥⲱ ΠΕΤΟΥΗΥ ΄ⲙⲙΟΕΙ ϤΟΥΗΥ ⲚΤⲘⲚΤΕΡΟ

83 ΠΕϪΕ Ιⳤ ²⁰ ϪΕ ⲚϨΙΚⲰΝ ⳤΕΟΥΟΝϨ ΕΒΟⲖ
ⲘΠΡⲰⲙΕ ΑΥⲱ ΠΟΥΟΕΙΝ ΕΤⲚϨΗΤΟΥ ϤϨΗΠ ΄ϨⲚ
ΘΙΚⲰΝ ⲘΠΟΥΟΕΙΝ ⲘΠΕΙⲱΤ ϤΝΑ΄ϬⲰⲖΠ ΕΒΟⲖ ΑΥⲱ
ΤΕϤϨΙΚⲰΝ ϨΗΠ ΄ΕΒΟⲖ ϨΙΤⲚ ΠΕϤΟΥΟΕΙΝ

84 ΠΕϪΕ Ιⳤ ⲚϨΟ²⁵ΟΥ ΕΤΕΤⲚΝΑΥ ΕΠΕΤⲚΕΙΝΕ
ϢΑΡΕΤⲚ΄ΡΑϢΕ ϨΟΤΑΝ ϪΕ ΕΤΕΤⲚϢΑΝΝΑΥ ΄
ΑΝΕΤⲚϨΙΚⲰΝ ⲚΤΑϨϢⲰΠΕ ϨΙ ΤΕΤΝΕ΄ϨΗ ΟΥΤΕ
ⲙΑΥⲙΟΥ ΟΥΤΕ ⲙΑΥΟΥⲰΝϨ ΄ΕΒΟⲖ ΤΕΤΝΑϤΙ ϨΑ
ΟΥΗΡ

85 ΠΕϪΕ Ιⳤ ϪΕ ³⁰ ⲚΤΑΑΔΑⲙ ϢⲰΠΕ ΕΒΟⲖ
ϨⲚΝΟΥΝΟϬ ΄ⲚΔΥΝΑⲙΙⳤ ⲙⲚ ΟΥΝΟϬ ⲘⲙⲚΤΡⲘⲙΑ΄Ο
ΑΥⲱ ⲘΠΕϤϢⲰΠΕ Ε[ϤⲘ]ΠϢΑ ⲘⲙⲰ΄ΤⲚ ΝΕΥΑϨΙΟⳤ
ⳌΑΡ ΠΕ [ΝΕϤΝΑϪΙ] Ϯ Π[Ε] ΄ΑΝ ⲘΠⲙΟΥ ΄

86 ΠΕϪΕ Ιⳤ ϪΕ [ΝΒΑϢΟΡ ΟΥ⁴⁸ⲚΤ]ΑΥ ΝΟΥ[Β]ΗΒ
ΑΥⲱ ⲚϨΑⲖΑΤΕ ΟΥⲚΤΑΥ ΄ⲙⲙΑΥ ⲘΠΕΥⲙΑϨ
ΠϢΗΡΕ ϪΕ ⲘΠΡⲰⲙΕ ΄ⲙⲚΤΑϤ ⲚⲚ[Ο]ΥⲙΑ ΕΡΙΚΕ
ⲚΤΕϤΑΠΕ ⲚϤ΄ⲘΤΟΝ Ⲙⲙ[Ο]Ϥ

79   A woman in the crowd said to him, "Fortunate are the womb that bore you and the breasts that fed you."

    He said to [her], "Fortunate are those who have heard the word of the father and have truly kept it. For there will be days when you will say, 'Fortunate are the womb that has not conceived and the breasts that have not given milk.' "

80   Jesus said, "Whoever has come to know the world has discovered the body, and whoever has discovered the body, of that person the world is not worthy."

81   Jesus said, "Let one who has become wealthy rule, and let one who has power renounce (it)."

82   Jesus said, "Whoever is near me is near the fire, and whoever is far from me is far from the kingdom."

83   Jesus said, "Images are visible to people, but the light within them is hidden in the image of the father's light. He will be disclosed, but his image is hidden by his light."

84   Jesus said, "When you see your likeness, you are happy. But when you see your images that came into being before you and that neither die nor become visible, how much you will bear!"

85   Jesus said, "Adam came from great power and great wealth, but he was not worthy of you. For had he been worthy, [he would] not [have tasted] death."

86   Jesus said, "[Foxes have] their dens and birds have their nests, but the child of humankind has no place to lay his head and rest."

87 ПЕϪΑϤ ＮϬΙ ӀС ϪЕ ΟΥΤΑΛΑΙ⁵ΠⲰΡΟΝ ΠΕ
ΠСⲰΜΑ ЕТАϢЕ ＮΟΥСⲰΜΑ · ΑΥⲰ ΟΥΤΑΛΑΙΠⲰΡΟС
ТЕ ТΨΥΧΗ ЕТАϢЕ · ＮΝΑЕΙ ΜΠСΝΑΥ

88 ПЕϪЕ ӀС ϪЕ ＮΑΓΓЕΛΟС · ΝΗΥ ϢΑΡⲰТＮ ΜＮ
ＮΠΡΟФΗТΗС ΑΥⲰ СЕΝΑϯ ΝΗТＮ ＮΝЕТЕΥＮТΗТＮСЕ
ΑΥⲰ ¹⁰ ＮТⲰТＮ ϩⲰТТΗΥТＮ ΝЕТＮТΟΥТΗΝЕ · ТΑΑΥ
ΝΑΥ ＮТЕТＮϪΟΟС ΝΗТＮ ϪЕ ΑϢ ＮϩΟΟΥ
ПЕТΟΥＮΝΗΥ ＮСЕϪΙ ПЕТЕ ПⲰΟΥ ·

89 ПЕϪЕ ӀС ϪЕ ЕТВЕ ΟΥ ТЕТＮЕΙⲰЕ ΜΠСΑ Ν'ΒΟΛ
ΜΠΠΟТΗΡΙΟΝ ТЕТＮΡΝΟЕΙ ΑΝ ϪЕ ¹⁵
ПЕΝТΑϩТΑΜΙΟ ΜΠСΑ ΝϩΟΥＮ ＮТΟϤ ΟΝ ·
ПЕΝТΑϤТΑΜΙΟ ΜΠСΑ ΝВΟΛ

90 ПЕϪЕ ӀΗС · ϪЕ ΑΜΗЕΙТＮ ϢΑΡΟЕΙ ϪЕ
ΟΥΧΡΗСТΟС · ПЕ ПΑΝΑϩВ ΑΥⲰ ТΑΜＮТϪΟЕΙС
ΟΥΡΜ̄'ΡΑϢ ТЕ ΑΥⲰ ТЕТΝΑϩЕ ΑΥΑΝΑΥПΑСΙС
ΝΗ²⁰ТＮ

91 ПЕϪΑΥ ΝΑϤ ϪЕ ϪΟΟС ЕΡΟΝ ϪЕ · ＮТΚ ΝΙΜ
ϢΙΝΑ ЕΝΑΡПΙСТЕΥЕ ЕΡΟΚ
ПЕ'ϪΑϤ ΝΑΥ ϪЕ ТЕТＮΡПΙΡΑϪЕ ΜΠϩΟ ＮТПЕ ·
ΜＮ ПΚΑϩ ΑΥⲰ ПЕТＮПЕТＮΜТΟ ЕВΟΛ ·
ΜΠЕТＮСΟΥⲰΝϤ ΑΥⲰ ПЕЕΙΚΑΙΡΟС ТЕ²⁵ТＮСΟΟΥΝ
ΑΝ ＮΡПΙΡΑϪЕ ΜΜΟϤ

92 ПЕϪЕ · ӀС ϪЕ ϢΙΝЕ ΑΥⲰ ТЕТΝΑϬΙΝЕ ΑΛΛΑ
ΝЕ'ТΑТЕТＮϪΝΟΥЕΙ ЕΡΟΟΥ ＮΝΙϩΟΟΥ ЕΜΠΙ'ϪΟΟΥ
ΝΗТＮ ΜФΟΟΥ ЕТΜΜΑΥ ТЕΝΟΥ · ЕϩΝΑΪ ЕϪΟΟΥ
ΑΥⲰ ТЕТＮϢΙΝЕ ΑΝ ＮСⲰ³⁰ΟΥ

93 ΜΠΡϯ ПЕТΟΥΑΑВ ＮΝΟΥϩΟΟΡ ϪЕΚΑС ·
ΝΟΥΝΟϪΟΥ ЕТΚΟΠΡΙΑ ΜΠΡΝΟΥϪЕ
ΝΜ'ΜΑΡΓΑΡΙТΗ[С Ｎ]ΝЕϢΑΥ ϢΙΝΑ ϪЕ ΝΟΥΑΑϤ ·
Ｎ̄ΛΑ[. . .]

94 [ПЕϪ]Е̣ ӀС ПЕТϢΙΝЕ ϤΝΑϬΙΝЕ · [ПЕТТⲰϩΜ̄
Е]ϩΟΥΝ СЕΝΑΟΥⲰΝ ΝΑϤ ³⁵

95 [ПЕϪЕ ӀС ϪЕ] ЕϢⲰПЕ ΟΥＮТΗТＮ ϩΟΜТ 49 ΜΠΡϯ
ЕТΜΗСЕ ΑΛΛΑ ϯ [ΜΜΟϤ] Μ̄ПЕТ[Е]ТΝΑϪΙТΟΥ ΑΝ
ＮТΟΟТϤ

87 Jesus said, "How miserable is the body that depends on a body, and how miserable is the soul that depends on these two."

88 Jesus said, "The messengers and the prophets will come to you and give you what is yours. You, in turn, give them what you have, and say to yourselves, 'When will they come and take what is theirs?'"

89 Jesus said, "Why do you wash the outside of the cup? Do you not understand that the one who made the inside is also the one who made the outside?"

90 Jesus said, "Come to me, for my yoke is easy and my mastery is gentle, and you will find rest for yourselves."

91 They said to him, "Tell us who you are so that we may believe in you."

He said to them, "You examine the face of heaven and earth, but you have not come to know the one who is in your presence, and you do not know how to examine this moment."

92 Jesus said, "Seek and you will find. In the past, however, I did not tell you the things about which you asked me then. Now I am willing to tell them, but you are not seeking them.

93 "Do not give what is holy to dogs, or they might throw them upon the manure pile. Do not throw pearls [to] swine, or they might . . . it [. . .]."

94 Jesus [said], "One who seeks will find; for [one who knocks] it will be opened."

95 [Jesus said], "If you have money, do not lend it at interest. Rather, give [it] to someone from whom you will not get it back."

96 ⲡ[ⲉⲍ]ⲉ ⲓ̅ⲥ̅ ⲍⲉ ⲧⲙ̅ⲛ̅ⲧⲉⲣⲟ ⲙ̅ⲡⲉⲓⲱⲧ ⲉⲥⲧⲛ̅ⲧⲱ[ⲛ
   ⲁⲩ]ⲥ̣ϩⲓⲙⲉ ⲁⲥϫⲓ ⲛ̅ⲟⲩⲕⲟⲩⲉⲓ ⲛ̅ⲥⲁⲉⲓⲣ ⲁ̣[ⲥϩ̣]ⲟⲡ̣ϥ
   ϩⲛ̅ ⁵ⲟⲩϣⲱⲧⲉ ⲁⲥⲁⲁϥ ⲛ̅ϩ̣ⲛ̅ⲛⲟ[ϭ ⲛ̅]ⲛⲟⲉⲓⲕ · ⲡⲉⲧⲉⲩⲙ̅
   ⲙⲁⲁϫⲉ ⲙ̅ⲙⲟϥ ⲙⲁ[ⲣⲉ]ϥⲥⲱⲧⲙ̅ ·

97 ⲡⲉϫⲉ ⲓ̅ⲥ̅ ϫⲉ ⲧⲙ̅ⲛ̅ⲧⲉⲣⲟ ⲙ̅ⲡⲉ[ⲓⲱⲧ ⲉ]ⲥⲧⲛ̅ⲧⲱⲛ
   ⲁⲩⲥϩⲓⲙⲉ ⲉⲥϥⲓ ϩⲁ ⲟⲩϭ̅ⲁ̅[ⲙⲉⲉⲓ] ⲉϥ̣ⲙⲉϩ ⲛ̅ⲛⲟⲉⲓⲧ
   ⲉⲥⲙⲟⲟϣⲉ ϩ[ⲓ ⲟⲩ]ϩⲓⲏ ¹⁰ⲉⲥⲟⲩⲏⲟⲩ ⲁⲡⲙⲁⲁϫⲉ
   ⲙ̅ⲡϭ̅ⲁ̅ⲙ̅[ⲉ]ⲉⲓ ⲟⲩⲱϭⲡ ⲁⲡⲛⲟⲉⲓⲧ ϣⲟⲩⲟ ⲛ̅ⲥⲱⲥ [ϩ]ⲓ̣
   ⲧⲉϩ̣ⲓ̣'ⲏ ⲛⲉⲥⲥⲟⲟⲩⲛ ⲁⲛ ⲡⲉ ⲛⲉⲙ̅ⲡⲉⲥⲉⲓⲙⲉ · ⲉϩⲓⲥⲉ
   ⲛ̅ⲧⲁⲣⲉⲥⲡⲱϩ ⲉϩⲟⲩⲛ ⲉⲡⲉⲥⲛⲉⲓ · ⲁⲥⲕⲁ ⲡϭ̅ⲁ̅ⲙⲉⲉⲓ
   ⲁⲡⲉⲥⲛⲧ ⲁⲥϩⲉ ⲉⲣⲟϥ ⲉϥ¹⁵ϣⲟⲩⲉⲓⲧ

98 ⲡⲉϫⲉ ⲓ̅ⲥ̅ ⲧⲙ̅ⲛ̅ⲧⲉⲣⲟ ⲙ̅ⲡⲉⲓⲱⲧ · ⲉⲥⲧⲛ̅ⲧⲱⲛ ⲉⲩⲣⲱⲙⲉ
   ⲉϥⲟⲩⲱϣ ⲉⲙⲟⲩⲧ · ⲟⲩⲣⲱⲙⲉ ⲙ̅ⲙⲉⲅⲓⲥⲧⲁⲛⲟⲥ
   ⲁϥϣⲱⲗⲙ ⲛ̅ⲧⲥⲏϥⲉ ϩⲙ̅ ⲡⲉϥⲛⲉⲓ ⲁϥϫⲟⲧⲥ̅ ⲛ̅ⲧϫⲟ
   ϫⲉ'ⲕⲁⲁⲥ ⲉϥⲛⲁⲉⲓⲙⲉ ϫⲉ ⲧⲉϥϭⲓϫ ⲛⲁⲧⲱⲕ ²⁰ⲉϩⲟⲩⲛ
   ⲧⲟⲧⲉ ⲁϥϩⲱⲧⲃ̅ ⲙ̅ⲡⲙⲉⲅⲓⲥⲧⲁⲛⲟⲥ ·

99 ⲡⲉϫⲉ ⲙ̅ⲙⲁⲑⲏⲧⲏⲥ ⲛⲁϥ ϫⲉ ⲛⲉⲕⲥⲛⲏⲩ · ⲙⲛ̅
   ⲧⲉⲕⲙⲁⲁⲩ ⲥⲉⲁϩⲉⲣⲁⲧⲟⲩ ϩⲓ ⲡⲥⲁ ⲛ̅ⲃⲟⲗ
   ⲡⲉϫⲁϥ ⲛⲁⲩ ϫⲉ ⲛⲉⲧⲛ̅ⲛⲉⲉⲓⲙⲁ · ⲉⲧⲣⲉ ⲙ̅ⲡⲟⲩⲱϣ
   ⲙ̅ⲡⲁⲉⲓⲱⲧ ⲛⲁⲉⲓ ⲛⲉ ²⁵ⲛⲁⲥⲛⲏⲩ ⲙⲛ̅ ⲧⲁⲙⲁⲁⲩ
   ⲛ̅ⲧⲟⲟⲩ ⲡⲉ ⲉⲧⲛⲁ ⲃⲱⲕ ⲉϩⲟⲩⲛ ⲉⲧⲙ̅ⲛ̅ⲧⲉⲣⲟ
   ⲙ̅ⲡⲁⲉⲓⲱⲧ ·

100 ⲁⲩⲧⲥⲉⲃⲉ ⲓ̅ⲥ̅ ⲁⲩⲛⲟⲩⲃ ⲁⲩⲱ ⲡⲉϫⲁⲩ ⲛⲁϥ · ϫⲉ
   ⲛⲉⲧⲏⲡ ⲁⲕⲁⲓⲥⲁⲣ ⲥⲉϣⲓⲧⲉ ⲙ̅ⲙⲟⲛ ⲛ̅ⲛ̅ϣⲱⲙ
   ⲡⲉϫⲁϥ ⲛⲁⲩ ϫⲉ ϯ ⲛⲁ ⲕⲁⲓⲥⲁⲣ ³⁰ⲛ̅ⲕⲁⲓⲥⲁⲣ ϯ
   ⲛⲁ ⲡⲛⲟⲩⲧⲉ ⲙ̅ⲡⲛⲟⲩⲧⲉ · ⲁⲩⲱ ⲡⲉⲧⲉ ⲡⲱⲉⲓ ⲡⲉ
   ⲙⲁⲧⲛ̅ⲛⲁⲉⲓϥ ·

101 ⲡⲉⲧⲁⲙⲉⲥⲧⲉ ⲡⲉϥⲉⲓ[ⲱⲧ] ⲁⲛ ⲙⲛ̅ ⲧⲉϥ'ⲙⲁⲁⲩ
   ⲛ̅ⲧⲁϩⲉ ϥⲛⲁϣⲣ̅ ⲙ̅[ⲁⲑⲏⲧ]ⲏⲥ ⲛⲁⲉⲓ ⲁⲛ · ⲁⲩⲱ
   ⲡⲉⲧⲁⲙ̅ⲣ̅ⲣⲉ ⲡⲉϥ[ⲉⲓⲱⲧ ⲁⲛ ⲙ]ⲛ̅ ⲧⲉϥ³⁵ⲙⲁⲁⲩ ⲛ̅ⲧⲁϩⲉ
   ϥⲛⲁϣⲣ̅ ⲙ̅[ⲁⲑⲏⲧⲏⲥ ⲛⲁ]ⲉⲓ ⲁⲛ ⲧⲁⲙⲁⲁⲩ ⲅⲁⲣ
   ⲛ̅ⲧⲁⲥ[. . . . . 50. .]ⲟⲗ ⲧⲁ[ⲙⲁⲁ]ⲩ ⲇⲉ ⲙ̅ⲙⲉ
   ⲁⲥϯ ⲛⲁⲉⲓ ⲙ̅ⲡⲱⲛϩ ·

96   Jesus [said], "The father's kingdom is like [a] woman. She took a little yeast, [hid] it in dough, and made it into large loaves of bread. Whoever has ears should hear."

97   Jesus said, "The [father's] kingdom is like a woman who was carrying a [jar] full of meal. While she was walking along [a] distant road, the handle of the jar broke and the meal spilled behind her [along] the road. She did not know it; she had not noticed a problem. When she reached her house, she put the jar down and discovered that it was empty."

98   Jesus said, "The father's kingdom is like a person who wanted to put someone powerful to death. While at home he drew his sword and thrust it into the wall to find out whether his hand would go in. Then he killed the powerful one."

99   The followers said to him, "Your brothers and your mother are standing outside."

He said to them, "Those here who do the will of my father are my brothers and my mother. They are the ones who will enter my father's kingdom."

100   They showed Jesus a gold coin and said to him, "Caesar's people demand taxes from us."

He said to them, "Give Caesar the things that are Caesar's, give God the things that are God's, and give me what is mine.

101   "Whoever does not hate [father] and mother as I do cannot be a [follower] of me, and whoever does [not] love [father and] mother as I do cannot be a [follower of] me. For my mother [. . .], but my true [mother] gave me life."

102 ΠΕϪΕ ΙⲤ [Ϫε Ο]ⲞⲨΟΕΙ ΝⲀⲨ ⲘⲪⲀⲢΙⲤⲀΙΟⲤ Ϫε '
ΕⲨΕΙΝⲈ [ⲚⲚ]ⲞⲨⲞⲨϩⲞⲢ ΕϤⲚⲔⲞⲦⲔ ϩΙϪⲚ ⲠⲞⲨⲞΝΕϤ
Ⲛϩ[Ⲛ]ΝΕϩⲞⲞⲨ Ϫε ⲞⲨⲦε ϤⲞⲨⲰⲘ ⲀⲚ ⁵ ⲞⲨⲦε ϤⲔ[Ⲱ]
ⲀⲚ ⲚⲚΕϩⲞⲞⲨ ΕⲞⲨⲰⲘ

103 ΠΕϪΕ ΙⲤ ' Ϫε ⲞⲨⲘⲀ[ⲔⲀ]ⲢΙⲞⲤ ⲠΕ ⲠⲢⲰⲘΕ ⲠⲀΕΙ
ΕⲦⲤⲞⲞⲨⲚ ' Ϫε ϩ[Ⲛ ⲀϢ] ⲘⲘΕⲢⲞⲤ ΕΝⲀⲎⲤⲦⲎⲤ ⲚⲎⲨ
ΕϩⲞⲨⲚ ' ϢΙΝⲀ [ΕϤ]ⲚⲀⲦⲰⲞⲨⲚ ⲚϤⲤⲰⲞⲨϩ
ⲚⲦΕϤⲘⲚⲦΕ[ⲢⲞ] ⲀⲨⲰ ⲚϤⲘⲞⲨⲢ ⲘⲘⲞϤ ΕϪⲚ
ⲦΕϤ¹⁰ⲦⲠΕ ϩ[Ⲁ] ⲦΕϩⲎ ΕⲘⲠⲀⲦⲞⲨΕΙ ΕϩⲞⲨⲚ

104 ΠΕϪⲀⲨ Ⲛ[Ι]Ⲥ Ϫε ⲀⲘⲞⲨ ⲚⲦⲚϢⲖⲎⲖ ⲘⲠⲞⲞⲨ '
ⲀⲨⲰ ⲚⲦⲚⲢⲚⲎⲤⲦΕⲨΕ
ΠΕϪΕ ΙⲤ Ϫε ⲞⲨ ⲄⲀⲢ ' ΠΕ ⲠΝⲞⲂΕ ⲚⲦⲀΕΙⲀⲀϤ Ⲏ
ⲚⲦⲀⲨϪⲢⲞ ΕⲢⲞΕΙ ' ϩⲚ ⲞⲨ ⲀⲖⲖⲀ ϩⲞⲦⲀⲚ
ΕⲢϢⲀⲚⲠⲚⲨⲘⲪΙⲞⲤ ΕΙ ¹⁵ ΕⲂⲞⲖ ϩⲘ ⲠⲚⲨⲘⲪⲰⲚ ⲦⲞⲦΕ
ⲘⲀⲢⲞⲨⲚⲎⲤⲦΕⲨΕ ⲀⲨⲰ ⲘⲀⲢⲞⲨϢⲖⲎⲖ

105 ΠΕϪΕ ΙⲤ Ϫε ⲠΕⲦΝⲀⲤⲞⲨⲰⲚ ⲠΕΙⲰⲦ ⲘⲚ ⲦⲘⲀⲀⲨ
ⲤΕΝⲀⲘⲞⲨⲦΕ ΕⲢⲞϤ Ϫε ⲠϢⲎⲢΕ ⲘⲠⲞⲢΝⲎ

106 ΠΕϪΕ ΙⲤ Ϫε ' ϩⲞⲦⲀⲚ ΕⲦΕⲦⲚϢⲀⲢ ⲠⲤΝⲀⲨ ⲞⲨⲀ
ⲦΕⲦΝⲀϢⲰ²⁰ⲠΕ ⲚϢⲎⲢΕ ⲘⲠⲢⲰⲘΕ ⲀⲨⲰ
ΕⲦΕⲦⲚϢⲀⲚϪⲞⲞⲤ Ϫε ⲠⲦⲞⲞⲨ ⲠⲰⲰΝΕ ΕⲂⲞⲖ
ϤΝⲀⲠⲰⲰΝΕ

107 ΠΕϪΕ ΙⲤ Ϫε ⲦⲘⲚⲦΕⲢⲞ ΕⲤⲦⲚⲦⲰⲚ ' ΕⲨⲢⲰⲘΕ
ⲚϢⲰⲤ ΕⲨⲚⲦⲀϤ ⲘⲘⲀⲨ ⲚϢΕ ⲚΕⲤⲞⲞⲨ ⲀⲞⲨⲀ
ⲚϩⲎⲦⲞⲨ ⲤⲰⲢⲘ ΕⲠⲚⲞϬ ⲠΕ ²⁵ ⲀϤⲔⲰ ⲘⲠⲤⲦΕⲮΙⲦ
ⲀϤϢΙⲚΕ ⲚⲤⲀ ⲠΙⲞⲨⲀ ' ϢⲀⲚⲦΕϤϩΕ ΕⲢⲞϤ
ⲚⲦⲀⲢΕϤϩΙⲤΕ ΠΕϪⲀϤ ' ⲘⲠΕⲤⲞⲞⲨ Ϫε ⲦⲞⲨⲞϢⲔ
ⲠⲀⲢⲀ ⲠⲤⲦΕⲮΙⲦ '

108 ΠΕϪΕ ΙⲤ Ϫε ⲠΕⲦⲀⲤⲰ ΕⲂⲞⲖ ϩⲚ ⲦⲀⲦⲀⲠⲢⲞ '
ϤΝⲀϢⲰⲠΕ ⲚⲦⲀϩΕ ⲀΝⲞⲔ ϩⲰ ⲦΝⲀϢⲰⲠΕ ³⁰ ΕΝⲦⲞϤ
ΠΕ ⲀⲨⲰ ΝΕⲐⲎⲠ ΝⲀⲞⲨⲰΝϩ ΕⲢⲞϤ '

102   Jesus said, "Damn the Pharisees, for they are like a dog sleeping in the cattle manger, for it does not eat or [let] the cattle eat."

103   Jesus said, "Fortunate is the person who knows where the robbers are going to enter, so that [he] may arise, bring together his estate, and arm himself before they enter."

104   They said to Jesus, "Come, let us pray today and let us fast."

Jesus said, "What sin have I committed, or how have I been undone? Rather, when the bridegroom leaves the wedding chamber, then let people fast and pray."

105   Jesus said, "Whoever knows the father and the mother will be called the child of a whore."

106   Jesus said, "When you make the two into one, you will become children of humanity, and when you say, 'Mountain, move from here,' it will move."

107   Jesus said, "The kingdom is like a shepherd who had a hundred sheep. One of them, the largest, went astray. He left the ninety-nine and sought the one until he found it. After he had gone to this trouble, he said to the sheep, 'I love you more than the ninety-nine.' "

108   Jesus said, "Whoever drinks from my mouth will become like me; I myself shall become that person, and the hidden things will be revealed to that person."

109 ⲡⲉϫⲉ ⲓ̅ⲥ̅ ϫⲉ ⲧⲙ̅ⲛ̅ⲧⲉⲣⲟ ⲉⲥⲧⲛ̅ⲧⲱⲛ ⲉⲩⲣⲱⲙⲉ
ⲉⲩⲛ̅ⲧⲁϥ ⲙ̅ⲙⲁⲩ ϩⲛ̅ ⲧⲉϥⲥⲱϣⲉ ⲛ̅ⲛⲟⲩⲉϩⲟ ⲉϥϩⲏⲡ
ⲉ]ϥⲟ ⲛ̅ⲁⲧⲥⲟⲟⲩⲛ ⲉⲣⲟϥ ⲁⲩⲱ ⲙ̅[ⲙⲛ̅ⲛⲥⲁ ⲧ]ⲣⲉϥⲙⲟⲩ
ⲁϥⲕⲁⲁϥ ⲙ̅ⲡⲉϥ³⁵[ϣⲏⲣⲉ ⲛⲉ]ⲡϣⲏⲣⲉ ⲥⲟⲟⲩⲛ ⲁⲛ
ⲁϥϥⲓ 51 ⲧⲥⲱϣⲉ ⲉⲧⲙ̅ⲙⲁⲩ ⲁϥⲧⲁⲁⲥ [ⲉⲃⲟ]ⲗ ⲁⲩⲱ
ⲡⲉ[ⲛ]ⲧⲁⲩⲧⲟⲟⲩⲥ ⲁϥⲉⲓ ⲉϥⲥⲕⲁⲉⲓ ⲁ[ϥϩⲉ]ⲉ̄ ⲁⲡⲉϩⲟ
ⲁϥⲁⲣⲭⲉⲓ ⲛ̅ϯ ϩⲟⲙⲧ ⲉⲧⲙⲛⲥⲉ ⲛ̅[ⲛⲉ]ⲧϥⲟⲩⲟⲱϣⲟⲩ ˈ

110 ⲡⲉϫⲉ ⲓ̅ⲥ̅ ϫⲉ ⲡⲉⲛⲧⲁϩϭⲓⲛⲉ ⲙ̅ⲡⲕⲟⲥⲙⲟⲥ ⁵ ⲛ̅ϥⲣ̅
ⲣⲙ̅ⲙⲁⲟ ⲙⲁⲣⲉϥⲁⲣⲛⲁ ⲙ̅ⲡⲕⲟⲥⲙⲟⲥ ˈ

111 ⲡⲉϫⲉ ⲓ̅ⲥ̅ ϫⲉ ⲙ̅ⲡⲏⲩⲉ ⲛⲁϭⲱⲗ ⲁⲩⲱ ⲡⲕⲁϩ ˈ
ⲙ̅ⲡⲉⲧⲛ̅ⲙ̅ⲧⲟ ⲉⲃⲟⲗ ⲁⲩⲱ ⲡⲉⲧⲟⲛϩ ⲉⲃⲟⲗ ϩⲛ̅ ˈ ⲡⲉⲧⲟⲛϩ
ϥⲛⲁⲛⲁⲩ ⲁⲛ ⲉⲙⲟⲩ
ⲟⲩⲭ ϩⲟⲧⲓ ⲉ̅ⲓ̅ⲥ̅ ˈ ϫⲱ ⲙ̅ⲙⲟⲥ ϫⲉ ⲡⲉⲧⲁϩⲉ ⲉⲣⲟϥ
ⲟⲩⲁⲁϥ ⲡⲕⲟⲥ¹⁰ⲙⲟⲥ ⲙ̅ⲡϣⲁ ⲙ̅ⲙⲟϥ ⲁⲛ

112 ⲡⲉϫⲉ ⲓ̅ⲥ̅ ϫⲉ ⲟⲩⲟⲉⲓ ˈⲛ̅ⲧⲥⲁⲣⲝ ⲧⲁⲉⲓ ⲉⲧⲟϣⲉ
ⲛ̅ⲧⲯⲩⲭⲏ ⲟⲩⲟⲉⲓ ˈⲛ̅ⲧⲯⲩⲭⲏ ⲧⲁⲉⲓ ⲉⲧⲟϣⲉ ⲛ̅ⲧⲥⲁⲣⲝ

113 ⲡⲉϫⲁⲩ ˈⲛⲁϥ ⲛ̅ϭⲓ ⲛⲉϥⲙⲁⲑⲏⲧⲏⲥ ϫⲉ ⲧⲙ̅ⲛ̅ⲧⲉⲣⲟ ˈ
ⲉⲥⲛ̅ⲛⲏⲩ ⲛ̅ⲁϣ ⲛ̅ϩⲟⲟⲩ
ⲉⲥⲛ̅ⲛⲏⲩ ⲁⲛ ϩⲛ̅ ⲟⲩ¹⁵ϭⲱϣⲧ ⲉⲃⲟⲗ ⲉⲩⲛⲁϫⲟⲟⲥ
ⲁⲛ ϫⲉ ⲉⲓⲥϩⲏⲛ̅ⲧⲉ ⲙ̅ⲡⲓⲥⲁ ⲏ ⲉⲓⲥϩⲏⲛ̅ⲧⲉ ⲧⲏ ⲁⲗⲗⲁ
ⲧⲙ̅ⲛ̅ⲧⲉⲣⲟ ˈⲙ̅ⲡⲉⲓⲱⲧ ⲉⲥⲡⲟⲣϣ ⲉⲃⲟⲗ ϩⲓϫⲙ̅ ⲡⲕⲁϩ
ⲁⲩⲱ ˈⲣ̅ⲣⲱⲙⲉ ⲛⲁⲩ ⲁⲛ ⲉⲣⲟⲥ

114 ⲡⲉϫⲉ ⲥⲓⲙⲱⲛ ⲡⲉⲧⲣⲟⲥ ˈⲛⲁⲩ ϫⲉ ⲙⲁⲣⲉⲙⲁⲣⲓϩⲁⲙ
ⲉⲓ ⲉⲃⲟⲗ ⲛ̅ϩⲏⲧⲛ̅ ²⁰ ϫⲉ ⲛ̅ⲥϩⲓⲟⲙⲉ ⲙ̅ⲡϣⲁ ⲁⲛ
ⲙ̅ⲡⲱⲛϩ
ⲡⲉϫⲉ ⲓ̅ⲥ̅ ˈ ϫⲉ ⲉⲓⲥϩⲏⲏⲧⲉ ⲁⲛⲟⲕ ϯⲛⲁⲥⲱⲕ ⲙ̅ⲙⲟⲥ
ϫⲉˈⲕⲁⲁⲥ ⲉⲉⲓⲛⲁⲁⲥ ⲛ̅ϩⲟⲟⲩⲧ ϣⲓⲛⲁ ⲉⲥⲛⲁϣⲱⲡⲉ
ϩⲱⲱⲥ ⲛ̅ⲟⲩⲡⲛ̅ⲁ̅ ⲉϥⲟⲛϩ ⲉϥⲉⲓⲛⲉ ⲙ̅ⲙⲱⲧⲛ̅ ⲛ̅ϩⲟⲟⲩⲧ
ϫⲉ ⲥϩⲓⲙⲉ ⲛⲓⲙ ⲉⲥⲛⲁⲁⲥ ²⁵ ⲛ̅ϩⲟⲟⲩⲧ ⲥⲛⲁⲃⲱⲕ
ⲉϩⲟⲩⲛ ⲉⲧⲙ̅ⲛ̅ⲧⲉⲣⲟ ˈⲛ̅ⲙ̅ⲡⲏⲩⲉ ˈ

ⲡⲉⲩⲁⲅⲅⲉⲗⲓⲟⲛ ˈ ⲡⲕⲁⲧⲁ ⲑⲱⲙⲁⲥ

109 Jesus said, "The kingdom is like a person who had a treasure hidden in his field but did not know it. And [when] he died, he left it to his [son]. The son [did] not know (about it). He took over the field and sold it. The buyer went plowing, [discovered] the treasure, and began to lend money at interest to whomever he wished."

110 Jesus said, "Let someone who has found the world and has become wealthy renounce the world."

111 Jesus said, "The heavens and the earth will roll up in your presence, and whoever is living from the living one will not see death."

Does not Jesus say, "Whoever has found oneself, of that person the world is not worthy"?

112 Jesus said, "Damn the flesh that depends on the soul. Damn the soul that depends on the flesh."

113 His followers said to him, "When will the kingdom come?"

"It will not come by watching for it. It will not be said, 'Look, here it is,' or 'Look, there it is.' Rather, the father's kingdom is spread out upon the earth, and people do not see it."

114 Simon Peter said to them, "Mary should leave us, for females are not worthy of life."

Jesus said, "Look, I shall guide her to make her male, so that she too may become a living spirit resembling you males. For every female who makes herself male will enter heaven's kingdom."

The Gospel According to Thomas

NOTES

PROLOGUE   "These are the hidden sayings that the living Jesus spoke": The incipit, or opening of the document, provides what is most likely the earlier version of the title. A second, later title is given at the end of the document: "The Gospel According to Thomas." A similar incipit opens another document from the Nag Hammadi library, Book of Thomas 138,1–4: "The hidden sayings that the savior spoke to Judas Thomas, which I, Mathaias, in turn recorded. I was walking, listening to them speak with each other."

"hidden sayings": or, "secret sayings," "obscure sayings" (so Bentley Layton, *The Gnostic Scriptures,* p. 380). The Nag Hammadi Secret Book of James 2,7–16 has James describe how such hidden sayings were recorded: "Now the twelve followers [were] all sitting together, recalling what the savior had said to each of them, whether in a hidden or an open manner, and organizing it in books. [And I] was writing what is in my [book]."

"the living Jesus": probably not the resurrected Christ as commonly understood, but rather Jesus who lives through his sayings.

"Judas Thomas the Twin": literally, "Didymos Judas Thomas." Didymos (from Greek) and Thomas (from Aramaic or Syriac) both mean "twin." Here Papyrus Oxyrhynchus 654.2–3 has simply, "[Judas, who is] also (called) Thomas." In the New Testament and early Christian literature mention is made of Judas the brother of Jesus and the apostle Thomas. Among Syrian Christians Judas Thomas is said to have been the twin brother of Jesus and is thus an ideal figure to function as guarantor of the sayings of Jesus. In Book of Thomas 138,4–10, Jesus says to Judas Thomas, "Brother Thomas, while you are still in the world, listen to me and I shall reveal to you what you have thought about in your heart. Now since it is said that you are my twin and my true friend, examine yourself and understand who you are, how you exist, and how you will come to be." Likewise, in Acts of Thomas 39, a donkey addresses Judas Thomas by saying, "Twin of Christ, apostle of the Most High and fellow initiate into the hidden word of Christ, who receives his hidden sayings . . ."

1   "he said": The speaker is thought most likely to be Jesus, although he could conceivably be Judas Thomas with an editorial note.

"Whoever discovers the interpretation of these sayings . . .": A similar concern for the salvific possibilities entailed in the study and interpretation of sayings is to be found in Jewish and Greco-Roman sources. Compare Sirach 39:1–3:

> But one who devotes one's soul and studies the law of the Most High will seek out the wisdom of all the ancients and will be concerned with prophecies. That person will keep in mind the discourse of reputable men and will go into the subtleties of parables. That person will seek out the hidden things of proverbs and will be occupied with the enigmas of parables.

In general, compare also John 8:51–52.

2   "Let one who seeks . . .": Versions of this saying are also known from the Gospel of the Hebrews and the Book of Thomas:

> One who has marveled will rule, and one who has ruled will rest. (Gospel of the Hebrews 4a)

> One who seeks will not stop until one finds. Having found, one will be astounded, and having been astounded, one will rule, and having ruled, one will rest. (Gospel of the Hebrews 4b)

> [Fortunate is] the wise person who has [sought truth, and] when it has been found, has rested upon it for ever, and has not been afraid of those who wish to trouble the wise person. (Book of Thomas 140,41–141,2)

Watch and pray. . . . And when you pray, you will find rest. . . .
For when you leave the pains and the passions of the body, you will
receive rest from the Good One, and you will rule with the king,
you united with him and he united with you, from now on, for ever
and ever. (Book of Thomas 145,8–16)

Papyrus Oxyrhynchus 654.8–9, like some of the passages cited above,
adds an additional stage to the process of seeking and finding: "and
[having ruled], one will [rest]." In general, compare also Matthew
7:7–8 (Q) [This designation of Q here and hereafter indicates that
this saying is regarded by scholars as having been included in the sayings gospel Q, the sayings source of the synoptic gospels Matthew
and Luke.]; Luke 11:9–10 (Q); the Nag Hammadi tractate Dialogue
of the Savior 20: "And [let] one who [knows] seek and find and rejoice." Such stages in the process of discovering wisdom are known
from Jewish wisdom literature. Thus Wisdom of Solomon 6:12,
17–20 outlines several stages involved in seeking and finding wisdom, and concludes that "the desire for wisdom leads to a
kingdom."

3   "If your leaders say to you . . .": This saying parodies announcements that the kingdom is in heaven above or in the underworld. In
Jewish wisdom literature, similar language is used to question the
place of wisdom (compare Job 28:12–14, 20–22; Baruch 3:29–32,
35–37; also Sirach 1:1–3; Deuteronomy 30:11–14; Romans 10:6–8).

"in the sea": Papyrus Oxyrhynchus 654.13 provides the variant
reading "under the earth."

"the kingdom is inside you and it is outside you": Compare Luke
17:20–21; Gospel of Thomas saying 113. Similar expressions are
known from the Manichaean Psalm Book, particularly 160,20–21:
"Heaven's kingdom, look, it is inside us, look, it is outside us. If we
believe in it, we shall live in it for ever."

"know yourselves": The well-known imperative "Know yourself" was among the Greek inscriptions at the oracular center dedi-
cated to Apollo at Delphi. It is discussed in Plutarch's essay On the E
at Delphi, and Plato's dialogue Alcibiades I. In Book of Thomas

138,7–21, Thomas is described as "the one who knows oneself." In early Christian literature, the formulation "know . . . be known" is attested in Galatians 4:8–9; 1 Corinthians 8:1–3; 13:12; the Nag Hammadi Gospel of Truth 19,32–33 ("They knew, they were known").

4   "The person old in days . . .": Several parallels to this saying are to be found in ancient literature. In Hippolytus, Refutation of All Heresies 5.7.20, the author states that the Naassene gnostics use the following citation from the Gospel of Thomas: "One who seeks will find me in children from seven years, for there, hidden in the fourteenth age, I am revealed." In Manichaean Psalm Book 192,2–3 occurs another parallel reading: "To the old people with gray hair the little children give instruction; those six years old give instruction to those sixty years old." And in Infancy Gospel of Thomas 7:3, Zacchaeus the teacher observes concerning his young pupil Jesus, "Friends, I think on my shame that I, being an old man, have been overcome by a child." In general, compare Matthew 11:25–27 (Q); Luke 10:21–22 (Q).

"a little child seven days old": This phrase probably indicates an uncircumcised child (a Jewish boy was to be circumcised on the eighth day), otherwise a child of the sabbath of the week of creation (compare Genesis 2:2–3).

"For many of the first will be last": Compare Matthew 20:16 (Q); Luke 13:30 (Q); Matthew 19:30; Mark 10:31. A similar statement of reversal is found in Barnabas 6:13: "Look, I make the last as the first."

"become a single one": This theme (becoming one, the two becoming one) occurs in Gospel of Thomas sayings 4, 22, 23, 48, and 106, as well as elsewhere in ancient literature. It is often associated with the primordial union achieved in sexual intercourse (for the Hebrews, heterosexual intercourse; for the Greeks, homosexual or heterosexual intercourse) as the two joined together at the beginning become one again (compare Genesis 2:21–24; Plato, Symposium 192DE). By extension, this oneness can designate an integrated existence beyond all the divisive features of human life.

5   "Know what is in front of your face . . .": A nearly identical version of this saying is given in Manichaean Kephalaia LXV 163,26–29, also as a saying of Jesus: "Understand what is in front of your face, and then what is hidden from you will be disclosed to you."

"For there is nothing hidden . . .": Compare Mark 4:22; Luke 8:17; Matthew 10:26 (Q); Luke 12:2 (Q). This portion of the saying is also found in Gospel of Thomas saying 6. Papyrus Oxyrhynchus 654.31 adds "and nothing buried that [will not be raised]." This additional statement has also been preserved as a saying of Jesus on a Christian burial shroud from Oxyrhynchus, dated to the fifth or sixth century.

6   "fast . . . pray . . . give to charity . . . diet . . .": The questions and answer address matters of Jewish or Jewish-Christian observance of rules of personal piety; compare Matthew 6:1–18; Didache 8:1–3. Saying 14 provides a more direct answer to these specific questions. Here Jesus seems to ignore the questions about outward piety and instead focuses upon the inner disposition of an individual.

"do not do what you hate": The negative formulation of the golden rule is common in Jewish and Christian literature.

"heaven": in Coptic, *pe.* Papyrus Oxyrhynchus 654.38 reads "truth" (Greek *alētheia,* equivalent to Coptic *me*).

"For there is nothing hidden . . .": See saying 5 and the note on "nothing hidden."

7   "Fortunate is the lion . . .": This riddle-like saying remains somewhat obscure. In ancient literature the lion could symbolize what is passionate and bestial. Hence this saying could suggest that although a human being may consume what is bestial or be consumed by it, there is hope for the human being—and the lion. In gnostic literature the ruler of this world (Yaldabaoth in the Secret Book of John) is sometimes said to look like a lion. This saying may ultimately be based upon statements in Plato, for instance his comparison (in Republic 588E–589B) of the soul to a being of three parts: a many-headed beast, a lion, and a human being. Plato recommends that the

human part of the soul (that is, reason) tame and nourish the leonine part (that is, the passion of the heart). For a full discussion of this saying, see Howard M. Jackson, *The Lion Becomes Man*.

"foul": or, "cursed."

8 "Humankind is like a wise fisherman . . .": the parable of the wise fisherman. Compare this parable with the parable of the fishing net in Matthew 13:47–50. Such parables about fishing are also found in Christian authors like Clement of Alexandria, "Macarius" of Syria, and Philoxenos of Mabbug. In Greek literature there is a similar fable (Babrius, Fable 4):

> A fisherman drew in a net that he had just cast, and it happened to be full of a variety of fish. The little one among the fish fled to the bottom and slipped out of the porous mesh, but the large one was caught and was laid stretched out in the boat. A way to be safe and clear of trouble is to be small, but seldom will you see a person large in reputation who escapes dangers.

"Humankind": or, "The human one"; literally, "The man." This term may refer either to humankind in general or to a given person (compare the child of humankind, that is, the "son of man," or the primordial human being, Adam) as the paradigm of humankind.

"with no difficulty": or, "with no effort."

"Whoever has ears . . .": This injunction to pay attention to the real meaning and interpretation occurs throughout early Christian literature.

9 "Look, the sower went out . . .": the parable of the sower. Compare Matthew 13:3–9; Mark 4:2–9; Luke 8:4–8. In each occurrence of the parable in the New Testament, the author has added an allegorical interpretation of the parable and placed it on the lips of Jesus (Matthew 13:18–23; Mark 4:13–20; Luke 8:11–15). Stories similar to the parable are known from Jewish and Greek literature. Thus Sirach 6:19 says, "Come to her (that is, Wisdom) like one who plows and sows, and wait for her good crops. For in her work you

will toil a little, and soon you will eat of her produce." In his Oratorical Instruction 5.11.24, Quintilian writes, "For instance, if you would say that the mind needs to be cultivated, you would use a comparison to the soil, which if neglected produces thorns and brambles but if cultivated produces a crop. . . ."

10   "I have thrown fire upon the world": Compare Luke 12:49 (Q?). The gnostic document Pistis Sophia 141 has Jesus utter a nearly identical saying. Jesus, who is called Aberamentho, says, "For this reason I said to you, 'I have come to throw fire upon the earth,' that is, I have come to cleanse the sins of the whole world with fire." See also Gospel of Thomas saying 16.

11   "This heaven will pass away . . .": Saying 11 is composed of four riddles about life in this world and beyond.

"This heaven . . . the one above it . . .": The two heavens will pass away. Presumably the third heaven (the realm of God; compare 2 Corinthians 12:2–4) will not. On the heavens passing away, compare Matthew 24:35; Mark 13:31; Luke 21:33; Matthew 5:18 (Q); Luke 16:17 (Q).

"During the days when you ate what is dead . . .": Compare Hippolytus, Refutation of All Heresies 5.8.32: "So they say, 'If you ate dead things and made them living, what will you do if you eat living things?' " On eating and making alive what is dead, see Gospel of Thomas saying 7 and the note on the lion being eaten; see also saying 60.

"On the day when you were one . . .": See Gospel of Thomas saying 4 and the note on becoming one.

12   "No matter where you are, you are to go to James the Just . . .": This saying affirms the leadership of James the Just. James the Just was the brother of Jesus and the leader of the church in Jerusalem until his death in 62 C.E. The stories about James told in the Memoirs of Hegesippus and preserved in Eusebius's Ecclesiastical History 2.23.4–7 illustrate something of his reputation:

James the brother of the master succeeded to (the leadership of) the church with the apostles. He was named Just by all from the times of the master until ours, since many were called James. This one was holy from his mother's womb. He did not drink wine or strong drink, nor did he eat meat; no razor touched his head, he did not anoint himself with oil, and he did not make use of the bath. He alone was allowed to enter into the sanctuary, for he did not wear wool but linen. He used to enter alone into the temple and be found kneeling and praying for forgiveness for the people, so that his knees grew dry like a camel's, because he constantly bowed down on his knees in worship of God and asked forgiveness for the people. So because of the extraordinary character of his righteousness he was called the Just and Oblias, that is, in Greek, rampart of the people and righteousness, as the prophets point out concerning him.

Secret Book of James 16,5–11 has James present himself as the person who sends the other followers of Jesus out on their missions: "So, not wishing to give them offense, I sent each one of them to a different place. But I myself went up to Jerusalem, praying that I might acquire a share with the beloved ones who will appear."

"for whose sake heaven and earth came into being": This is an expression used in Jewish literature to praise someone.

13 "Compare me to something . . .": This dialogue is the version in the Gospel of Thomas of a story that is told in the synoptic gospels (Matthew 16:13–23; Mark 8:27–33; Luke 9:18–22), and that recounts in those gospels what happened on the road to Caesarea Philippi. In the New Testament versions (especially Matthew), Peter is the leading character in the story; in the Gospel of Thomas, it is Thomas who comes to insight.

"messenger": or, "angel."

"I am not your teacher. Because you have drunk, you have become intoxicated . . .": or, "I am not your teacher, for you have drunk and have become intoxicated . . ." On becoming intoxicated by drinking from living water, see Odes of Solomon 11:6–9.

"three sayings": or, "three words." These three sayings or words are unknown, but presumably they are powerful and provocative sayings, since stoning (mentioned by Thomas) was the Jewish punishment for blasphemy. Worth noting are the following examples of three words or sayings: Hippolytus, *Refutation of All Heresies* 5.8.4, cites the three words Kaulakau, Saulasau, Zeesar, derived from the Hebrew of Isaiah 28:10, 13; *Pistis Sophia* 136 mentions Yao Yao Yao, the Greek version (with three letters, given three times) of the ineffable name of God; the *Gospel of Bartholomew* and the *Secret Book of John* provide statements of identification with the father, the mother (or the holy spirit), and the son. *Acts of Thomas* 47 and Manichaean *Kephalaia* I 5,26–34 also refer to the three sayings or words but do not disclose precisely what they were.

"fire will come from the rocks . . .": Compare *Gospel of Bartholomew* 2:5: "Blessed Mary said to him, 'Why do you ask me about these mysteries? If I begin to make them known, fire will come out of my mouth and consume the whole world.'"

14 "If you fast . . .": Note the questions raised by the disciples in saying 6.

"walk through the countryside": literally, "walk in the places."

"when people receive you, eat . . . heal . . ." Compare Matthew 10:8 (Q); Luke 10:8–9 (Q); 1 Corinthians 10:27.

"For what goes into your mouth will not defile you . . .": Compare Matthew 15:11; Mark 7:15.

15 "one who was not born of woman": that is, a person who is not of human birth.

"That is your father": Manichaean *Psalm Book* 121,25–33 also declares an identity between the father and the one not of human birth:

[I] hear that you are in your father (and) your father is hidden in [you]. My master. [When I say], "The son was [begotten]," I [shall] find [the] father also beside him. My master. Shall I destroy a kingdom that I may provide a womb of a woman? My master. Your holy womb is the luminaries that conceive you. In the trees and the fruit is your holy body. My master Jesus.

In the New Testament, compare John 10:30.

16 "Perhaps people think that I have come to impose peace . . .": Compare Matthew 10:34–36 (Q); Luke 12:49 (Q?), 50, 51–53 (Q). See also Gospel of Thomas saying 10; Matthew 10:21–22; Mark 13:12–13; Luke 21:16–19; Micah 7:6.

"they will stand": The theme of standing, or stability, is found in Gospel of Thomas sayings 16, 18, 23, 28, and 50. According to accounts concerning the famous gnostic teacher Simon the Magician, he referred to himself as the standing one. The Nag Hammadi tractate entitled Three Steles of Seth applies this epithet to the divine, and adds that God "was first to stand" (119,17–18). This theme is discussed fully in Michael A. Williams, *The Immovable Race*.

"alone": or, "solitary." This word (*monachos*) is found in sayings 16, 49, and 75. The term may indicate one who is unique, solitary, or lonely, one who is unmarried, or (later, in a technical sense) a monk.

17 "I shall give you what no eye has seen . . .": This saying is also cited in 1 Corinthians 2:9, perhaps as a wisdom saying in use among the enthusiasts of Corinthians. Compare Isaiah 64:4. The saying occurs frequently in Jewish and Christian literature, and sometimes it is said to come from the Apocalypse of Elijah or the Secrets (or, apocrypha) of Elijah. At other times it is said to be a saying of Jesus. A variant of the saying is also found in Plutarch, How the Young Person Should Study Poetry 17E: "And let these (words) of Empedocles be at hand: 'Thus these things are not to be seen by men, nor heard, nor comprehended with the mind.' . . ." The parallels have been collected by Michael E. Stone and John Strugnell, *The Books of Elijah: Parts 1–2*, pp. 41–73.

18 "The followers said . . .": Jesus' followers raise a similar question in Matthew 24:3; Mark 13:3–4; Luke 21:7.

"For where the beginning is . . .": To return to the beginning is to attain the end; compare Gospel of Thomas saying 49. Also compare Manichaean Psalm Book 155,9–12: "Holy ones, rejoice with me, for I have returned again to my beginning. I [have] received my clean garments, my robes that do not become old. I have rejoiced in their joy, I have been glad in their gladness, [I have rested] in their rest from everlasting to everlasting." Secret Book of John II 9,5–8 makes a similar point: "And he spoke, and glorified and praised the invisible spirit, saying, 'Because of you everything has come into being, and everything will return to you.'"

"one who stands": See saying 16 and the note on standing.

19   "Fortunate is one who came into being . . .": Perhaps compare John 8:58. Lactantius, Divine Institutes 4.8, writes, "For we especially testify that he (that is, Christ) was born twice, first in the spirit and afterwards in the flesh. Whence it is thus said in Jeremiah, 'Before I formed you in the womb, I knew you.' And also in the same work, 'Fortunate is one who existed before being born,' which happened to no one else except Christ." Irenaeus, Proof of the Apostolic Preaching 43, offers the following: "And again he says, 'Fortunate is one who existed before becoming human.'" Gospel of Thomas saying 19 may not be referring to Christ at all in this beatitude. Rather, the sense of the saying could be that anyone who existed before being born should be declared fortunate. Compare the saying of Jesus in the Nag Hammadi Gospel of Philip 64,10–12: "Fortunate is one who exists before coming into being. For one who exists has been and will be."

"these stones": Stones performing acts of service are also mentioned in Matthew 3:9 (Q); Luke 3:8 (Q); Gospel of Thomas saying 77; Habakkuk 2:11. Note also Matthew 4:3 (Q); Luke 4:3 (Q); 19:40.

"five trees in paradise": The five trees in paradise are mentioned frequently in gnostic texts, ordinarily without explanation or elaboration. In Manichaean Psalm Book 161,17–29, it is said that various features of life and faith are put together in groups of five. This section opens with the statement, "For [five] are the trees that are in paradise [. . .] in summer and winter." On the trees in paradise according to Genesis, see Genesis 2:9.

20 "It is like a mustard seed . . .": the parable of the mustard seed. Compare Matthew 13:31–32 (Q); Luke 13:18–19 (Q); Mark 4:30–32. For Hebrew sayings that make similar comparisons, see Ezekiel 17:22–23; Daniel 4:20–21. John Dominic Crossan, *The Historical Jesus,* pp. 276–79, notes that the mustard plant could be either a weed growing wild in a field or a domesticated plant with a tendency to grow out of control.

"a mustard seed. <It> is the smallest": or, "a mustard seed, the smallest" (restoring to read <es>sob^{e}k).

21 "They are like little children": Followers of Jesus are commonly compared to children in the New Testament, the Gospel of Thomas, and other early Christian literature.

"They take off their clothes": They remove their garments of flesh when they are liberated from their bodies; see Gospel of Thomas saying 37. Here note may also be made of Hippolytus, Refutation of All Heresies 5.8.44:

> For this, he says, is "the gate of heaven," and this is "<the> house of God," where the good God dwells alone, into which no one will enter, he says, who is unclean, psychical, or carnal, but it is reserved for the spiritual alone, where it is necessary for them, when they have come there, to cast off their clothing and all become bridegrooms, having been made male through the virgin spirit.

"to give it back to them, and they return their field to them": or, "to give it back to them and return their field to them."

"if the owner of a house knows that a thief is coming . . .": Compare Gospel of Thomas saying 103; Matthew 24:43 (Q); Luke 12:39 (Q).

"When the crop ripened . . .": Compare Mark 4:29; Joel 3:13.

"with sickle in hand": literally, "with his sickle in his hand."

"Whoever has ears . . .": This injunction to pay attention to the real meaning and interpretation occurs throughout early Christian literature.

22   "Then shall we enter the kingdom as babies?": Compare the similarly naive question of Nicodemus, who also functions literarily as "straight man" for Jesus in John 3:4.

"When you make the two into one . . .": Versions of this saying are known from several early Christian documents, among them the Gospel of the Egyptians, 2 Clement, and the Martyrdom of Peter:

> Therefore Cassianus says, "When Salome inquired when the things about which she had asked would be known, the master said, 'When you have trampled the garment of shame, and when the two become one, and the male with the female is neither male nor female.'" Now first of all, we do not have this saying in the four gospels handed down to us but rather in the (Gospel) according to the Egyptians. (Gospel of the Egyptians 5)

> For when the master himself was asked by someone when his kingdom would come, he said, "When the two will be one, and the outer like the inner, and the male with the female neither male nor female." Now the two are one when we speak truth to each other and there is one soul in two bodies with no hypocrisy. And by the inside like the outside he means this: He means that the inside is the soul and he means that the outside is the body. Therefore, just as your body is visible, so also let your soul be evident in good works. And by the male with the female neither male nor female he means this, that when a brother sees a sister he should think of her not at all as female, nor should she think of him at all as male. When you do these things, he says, my father's kingdom will come. (2 Clement 12:2–6)

> Concerning this the master says in a mystery, "If you do not make what is on the right like what is on the left and what is on the left like what is on the right, and what is above like what is below, and what is behind like what is before, you will not recognize the kingdom." (Martyrdom of Peter 9)

In this last passage Peter, who is crucified upside-down, compares his position with that of the first human being. Philip makes a similar comparison in Acts of Philip 140, where he also cites a variant of this saying. For a New Testament statement bearing some resemblance to this saying, see Galatians 3:27–28. On the two becoming one, see saying 4 and the note on becoming one.

"and when you make male and female": or, "and in order that you may make male and female."

"an image in place of an image": Compare the gnostic account of creation in the Nag Hammadi Letter of Peter to Philip 136,5–11: "So he, the arrogant one, became haughty because of the praise of the powers. He became a rival, and he wanted [to] make an image in place [of an image] and a form in place of a form."

23 "I shall choose you, one from a thousand . . .": Compare Deuteronomy 32:30; Ecclesiastes 7:28. In other early Christian texts, the same expression occurs; for example, Pistis Sophia 134: "The savior answered and said to Mary, 'I say to you, there will be found one in a thousand, two in ten thousand, for the completion of the mystery of the first mystery.'" Again, compare Irenaeus, Against Heresies 1.24.6: "Moreover, not many can understand these things, but one in a thousand and two in ten thousand." This expression may also be found in the prayers of the Mandaeans, the gnostics from the area of the lower Tigris and Euphrates rivers.

"they will stand as a single one": See sayings 4 and 16 and the notes on becoming one and standing.

24 "Whoever has ears . . .": This injunction to pay attention to the real interpretation occurs throughout early Christian literature.

"There is light . . .": In general, compare Matthew 6:22–23 (Q); Luke 11:34–35 (Q), 36 (Q?). A similar discussion occurs in a fragmentary passage from Dialogue of the Savior 8.

"person of light": It is possible to suggest that a play on two Greek words meaning "human being" and "light" (*phōs* and *phōs,* accented differently in the Greek) may account for a uniting of these concepts in a "person of light." This very play on words is found in Zosimos of Panopolis, On the Letter Omega. In gnosticizing documents it is commonly maintained that a divine spark of light enlightens the life of the person of knowledge.

"it . . . it . . . it . . .": or, "he . . . he . . . he . . ."

25 "Love your brother . . .": Compare Matthew 22:39; Mark 12:31, 33; Luke 10:27; Leviticus 19:18. Gospel of the Hebrews 5 has the savior say, "And never rejoice except when you look upon your brother with love," and Didache 2:7 commands that "some you shall love more than your soul."

"soul": or, "life," even "self."

26 "You see the speck . . .": Compare Matthew 7:3–5 (Q); Luke 6:41–42 (Q). In the Babylonian Talmud, 'Arakin 16b, a similar saying is recounted: "It was taught: Rabbi Tarfon said, 'I wonder whether there is a person of this generation who accepts admonition? If someone says to him, "Remove the chip from between your eyes (or, eye teeth)," he would say to him, "Remove the beam from between your eyes (or, eye teeth).""'"

27 "If you do not fast from the world . . .": Clement of Alexandria, Miscellanies ("Stromateis") 3.15.99.4, incorporates a beatitude with similar content: "Those who have castrated themselves from all sin for the sake of heaven's kingdom are fortunate: They are the ones who fast from the world." Fasting from the world means abstaining from the material things that the world has to offer; keeping the sabbath a sabbath seems to imply that one should rest in a truly significant way and separate oneself from worldly concerns. Thus "Macarius" of Syria is cited by Aelred Baker ("Pseudo-Macarius and the Gospel of Thomas," p. 220) as making the same sort of statement: "For the soul that is considered worthy from the shameful and foul reflections keeps the sabbath a true sabbath and rests a true rest. . . . To all the souls that obey and come he gives rest from these . . . impure reflections . . . , (the souls) keeping the sabbath a true sabbath."

The words "observe the sabbath as a sabbath" in saying 27 could also be taken to derive from the idiom "keep the sabbath (in reference to) the sabbath," as in the Septuagint. Further, since the Coptic employs two different spellings for the word translated "sabbath" in saying 27 (*sambaton* and *sabbaton*), it is conceivable—but probably too subtle—that the text could be translated "observe the (whole) week as the sabbath"; compare Tertullian, Against the Jewish People 4: "We ought to keep a sabbath from all servile work always, and not only every seventh day, but all the time."

28 "I took my stand": See saying 16 and the note on standing.

"in flesh I appeared to them": Compare John 1:14; 1 Timothy 3:16; also Proverbs 1:20–33 and Baruch 3:37, in which passages Wisdom is said to appear to people.

"drunk": In gnostic and other texts, the person who is ignorant and without knowledge is frequently said to be drunk. Compare, for instance, the Hermetic text Poimandres 27, in which this proclamation is given: "O you nations, you earth-born men, who have given yourselves up to drunkenness and sleep and ignorance of God, become sober and stop carousing, enchanted by irrational sleep."

29 "If the flesh came into being . . .": This saying expresses surprise at the close relationship between the spirit, the immortal dimension of human beings, and the flesh or body. Inasmuch as the saying intimates that the spirit within may actually exist for the benefit and salvation of the body, it resembles saying 7.

30 "Where there are three deities . . .": Papyrus Oxyrhynchus 1.23–30 has been reconstructed to read as follows: "[Jesus says], 'Where there are [three, they are without] God, and where there is only [one], I say, I am with that one. Lift up the stone, and you will find me there. Split the piece of wood, and I am there.'" The conclusion of this saying is presented as a part of saying 77 in the Nag Hammadi Gospel of Thomas. See Harold W. Attridge, "The Original Text of Gos. Thom., Saying 30." In the New Testament,

compare Matthew 18:19–20. In other early Christian literature, compare Ephraem Syrus, Exposition on the Harmony of the Gospel 14: "Where there is one, there also am I, or someone might be sad from lonely things, since he himself is our joy and he himself is with us. And where there are two, there also shall I be, since his mercy and grace overshadow us. And when we are three, we assemble just as in church, which is the body of Christ perfected and his image expressed." In a medieval inquisition record that recounts the confession of Peter Maurinus, it is said that "where there was one little one of his, he himself would be with him, and where there were two, similarly, and where there were three, in the same way."

31   "A prophet . . .": Compare Matthew 13:57; Mark 6:4; Luke 4:23–24; John 4:44.

32   "A city . . .": Compare Matthew 5:14; 7:24–25 (Q); Luke 6:47–48 (Q).

33   "What you will hear in your ear . . .": Compare Matthew 10:27 (Q); Luke 12:3 (Q).

"in the other ear": This may represent an instance of dittography (that is, inadvertently writing something twice), or the phrase may refer to someone else's ear or even one's own "inner" ear. Here Papyrus Oxyrhynchus 1.41–42 merely reads, "Jesus says, '<What> you hear in one ear of yours [proclaim . . .].'" A fairly esoteric understanding of a version of the saying is assumed by Clement of Alexandria in his Miscellanies 6.15.124.5–6:

> "And what you hear in the ear"—that is, in a hidden manner and in a mystery, for such things are said, figuratively, to be spoken in the ear—"proclaim," he says, "upon the rooftops," receiving nobly and delivering loftily and explaining the scriptures according to the canon of truth. For neither prophecy nor the savior himself declared the divine mysteries in a simple manner, so as to be easily comprehended by ordinary people, but rather he spoke in parables.

"For no one lights a lamp . . .": Compare Matthew 5:15 (Q); Luke 11:33 (Q); Mark 4:21; Luke 8:16.

34　"If a blind person . . .": Compare Matthew 15:14 (Q); Luke 6:39 (Q).

35　"You cannot enter . . .": Compare Matthew 12:29 (Q?); Mark 3:27; Luke 11:21–22 (Q?).

36　"Do not worry . . .": Compare Matthew 6:25–33 (Q), 34; Luke 12:22–31 (Q), 32. In a manner somewhat like that of Q, Papyrus Oxyrhynchus 655.1–17 gives a fuller statement:

> [Jesus says, "Do not worry], from morning [to evening nor] from [evening to] morning, either [about] your [food], what [you will] eat, [or] about [your clothing], what you [will] wear. [You are much] better than the lilies, which do not card or [spin]. As for you, when you have no garment, what [will you put] on? Who might add to your stature? That very one will give you your garment."

The Greco-Roman author Epictetus makes similar observations, in his Discourses 1.9.9 and 1.14.3, when he advises the philosopher to be at least as self-reliant as animals are, and he notes the regular way in which plants go through their cycles, "as if from a command of God."

37　"When you strip . . .": Compare Gospel of the Egyptians 5 (cited at saying 22); Hippolytus, Refutation of All Heresies 5.8.44 (cited at saying 21); Gospel of Thomas saying 21; especially Manichaean Psalm Book 99,26–30; "The saying (or, word) of Jesus the redeemer came to [me (?), as] is appropriate: 'The vain garment of this flesh I have stripped off, and I am saved and purified; I have caused the clean feet of my soul to trample upon it confidently; with the gods that are clothed with Christ have I stood in line.'" This last text, like saying 37, combines references to stripping and to trampling. In his article "The Garments of Shame," Jonathan Z. Smith argues that such stripping and trampling reflect early Christian baptismal practice. Quotations from the Gospel of Philip, Cyril of Jerusalem, and Augustine may support this interpretation:

> The living water is a body. It is fitting that we put on the living person. For this reason, when one is about to go down to the water, one strips so that one may put on that one (that is, the living person). (Gospel of Philip 75,21–25)

> So then, once you entered, you took off your garment, and this was an image of taking off the old person with its deeds. Having taken this off, you were naked. . . . How marvelous! You were naked in the sight of all and were not ashamed. For truly you were bearing a copy of the first-formed Adam, who in paradise was naked and not ashamed. (Cyril of Jerusalem, Mystagogical Catechesis 2.2)

> In such great masses of troubles, then, clothe yourselves with goatskin and humble your souls through fasting. What is denied to pride is restored to humility. Indeed, when you were examined and the one who instigates flight and desertion was duly rebuked by the omnipotence of the awesome trinity, you were not clothed with goatskin, yet your feet stood mystically upon it. Vices and skins of she-goats are to be trampled under foot; cloth from perverse kids is to be torn apart. (Augustine, Sermon 216.10–11, on prebaptismal instruction)

As is hinted at by Cyril of Jerusalem, the ultimate source of these motifs of stripping and trampling may be the book of Genesis (2:25; 3:14–15). In their article "Stripped Before God," April D. De Conick and Jarl Fossum concur that these motifs derive from the Genesis story, but they challenge Smith's suggestion that saying 37 provides an interpretation of early Christian baptism. Instead, they note that stripping commonly refers to the removal of the fleshly body (compare saying 21), and trampling clothes in a childlike way may be understood as the renunciation of the flesh, so that the one who strips off and tramples upon clothes behaves like a child and achieves a childlike purity and innocence. De Conick and Fossum observe that in two Nag Hammadi documents, On the Anointing and Reality of the Rulers ("Hypostasis of the Archons"), such trampling is said to aid in overcoming the world and the powers of the world, and in these two texts trampling is discussed in the context of anointing. Thus, they conclude, saying 37 describes the means employed (perhaps including anointing) for embracing purity and attaining a vision of the divine.

"When you strip without being ashamed": It is also possible to translate the Coptic, "When you strip off your shame." The Greek of Papyrus Oxyrhynchus 655.22–23, however, must be translated, "When you strip and are not ashamed."

38   "Often you have desired to hear . . .": Compare Matthew 13:17 (Q); Luke 10:24 (Q); 17:22; John 7:33–36. Variants of this saying occur in Irenaeus, the Manichaean Psalm Book, the Acts of John, and Cyprian:

> Often I have desired to hear one of these sayings (or, words), and I have had no one to tell (me). (Irenaeus, Against Heresies 1.20.2)

> I have something to say, I have no one to whom to say it. (Manichaean Psalm Book 187,28–29)

> John, there must be one person to hear these things from me, for I need one who is going to hear. (Acts of John 98)

> For a time will come and you will seek me, both you and those who will come after, to hear a word of wisdom and understanding, and you will not find (me). (Cyprian, Three Books of Testimonies to Quirinus 3.29)

"you will seek me and you will not find me": According to Proverbs 1:23–28, Wisdom speaks and is ignored, and thereafter people who seek her do not find her.

39   "The Pharisees and the scribes . . .": Compare Matthew 23:13 (Q); Luke 11:52 (Q); Pseudo-Clementine Recognitions 2.30.1: "Similarly also he attacks the scribes and Pharisees during the last period of his teaching, charging them with improper actions and in-

correct teaching, and with hiding the key of knowledge that they received, handed down from Moses, by which the gate of the heavenly kingdom may be opened."

"taken": or, "received."

"be as shrewd as snakes . . .": Compare Matthew 10:16; Ignatius, Polycarp 2:2 "Be as shrewd as a snake in all things and as innocent as the dove for ever." Comparisons to snakes and doves are also known from the Midrash Rabbah, Song of Songs.

40 "A grapevine has been planted . . .": Compare Matthew 15:13; John 15:5–6; Isaiah 5:1–7. See also the parable of the planted weeds in Gospel of Thomas saying 57 and Matthew 13:24–30, and the parable of the grapevine and the weeds in Book of Thomas 144,19–36 (if the sun shines on a grapevine and it prospers, it will dominate the weeds; otherwise the master must pull them out).

41 "Whoever has something . . .": Compare Matthew 13:12; Mark 4:24–25; Luke 8:18; Matthew 25:29 (Q); Luke 19:26 (Q).

"in hand": literally, "in his hand."

42 "Be passersby": This saying may also be translated "Be wanderers"; compare descriptions in early Christian literature of wandering teachers and missionaries. Another possible but less likely translation is, "Come into being as you pass away"; compare the use of the same word *parage* as "pass away" in the first riddle in saying 11, and other statements similar to this translation of saying 42 (for example, 2 Corinthians 4:16; Acts of John 76: "Die so that you may live"). Tjitze Baarda, "Jesus Said: Be Passers-By," suggests yet another possible translation, "Be Hebrews," with the understanding of Philo of Alexandria that the word "Hebrews" may be taken as "migrants." A medieval author, Petrus Alphonsi, preserves a saying much like saying 42 in his Clerical Instruction: "This world is, as it were, a bridge. Therefore, pass over it, only do not lodge there." A very similar saying attributed to Jesus is preserved in the form of an Arabic inscription at the site of a mosque at Fatehpur-Sikri, India.

43   "You do not know . . .": Compare John 14:8–11.

"they love the tree . . .": Compare Luke 6:43–44 (Q); Matthew 7:16a, 16b (Q), 17, 18 (Q), 19–20; 12:33a–b, 33c (Q).

44   "Whoever blasphemes . . .": Compare Matthew 12:31–32 (Q); Luke 12:10 (Q); Mark 3:28–29.

45   "Grapes are not harvested . . .": Compare Luke 6:43–45 (Q); Matthew 7:16a, 16b (Q), 17, 18 (Q), 19–20; 12:33a–b, 33c (Q), 34a, 34b–35 (Q); James 3:12.

"the storehouse": literally, "his storehouse."

"the corrupt storehouse in the heart": literally, "his corrupt storehouse in his heart."

46   "From Adam to John the Baptist . . .": Compare Matthew 11:11 (Q); Luke 7:28 (Q).

"be averted": literally, "be broken"; the person's gaze turns away in deference or respect.

47   "And a servant cannot serve two masters . . .": Compare Matthew 6:24 (Q); Luke 16:13 (Q); 2 Clement 6:1: "And the master says, 'No servant can serve two masters.' If we wish to serve both God and mammon, it is harmful for us."

"No person drinks aged wine . . .": Compare Matthew 9:17; Mark 2:22; Luke 5:37–39.

"An old patch . . .": Compare Matthew 9:16; Mark 2:21; Luke 5:36.

48   "If two make peace with each other . . .": Compare Gospel of Thomas saying 106; Matthew 18:19; 17:20b (Q); Luke 17:6b (Q); Matthew 21:21; Mark 11:23; Didascalia 3.7.2 (Latin): ". . . since it is written in the gospel, 'If two come together into one and they say to this mountain, "Get up and throw yourself into the sea," it will happen.' " On faith moving mountains, compare 1 Corinthians 13:2.

"two . . . in a single house": See saying 4 and the note on be-coming one.

49   "alone and chosen": The same combination of these two terms used to describe those who enter the kingdom is to be found in Dialogue of the Savior 1–2.

"alone": or, "solitary." See saying 16 and the note on "alone."

"For you have come from it . . .": The end to be attained coin-cides with the beginning. See saying 18 and the note on where the beginning is; the note includes a citation of Manichaean Psalm Book 155,9–12 and Secret Book of John II 9,5–8.

50   "If they say to you . . .": This saying is one of the most overtly mythological sayings in the Gospel of Thomas. Much of what is recounted here is familiar from ancient descriptions of the life of the soul, particularly gnostic descriptions (for example, the Hymn of the Pearl in Acts of Thomas 108–13). Many of the specific features of this saying resemble the myth that is presented in more detail in the Secret Book of John. The question asked and the answers given in the saying also recall accounts of the heavenly powers interrogat-ing the soul as it passes through the spheres of heaven. According to Irenaeus, Against Heresies 1.21.5, the soul is to respond, "I am a child of the father, the father who is preexistent, a child, moreover, in the one who is preexistent. . . . I trace my origin from the one who is preexistent and back to what is my own, from where I have come." Then, Irenaeus observes, it is thought that the soul can es-cape from the powers.

"the light came into being . . .": Compare John 1:1–5, 9–14.

"established [itself]": or, "stood." On the motif of standing see saying 16 and the note on standing.

"its children": Compare John 12:36a.

"motion and rest": Compare Genesis 1:1–2:4a: in 1:2 the spirit moves, in 1:28 living things move, and in 2:2 God rests. According to the Secret Book of John II 19,22–33; 26,26–32, the inanimate body of Adam moved only when the demiurge Yaldabaoth breathed spirit into his face. Eventually the soul, thus empowered, would be able to find rest.

51   "What you look for has come . . .": The new world has already come. Compare Luke 17:20–21; Gospel of Thomas saying 113; John 3:18–19; 5:25; 2 Timothy 2:17–18. On the resurrection as something that has occurred already, compare the Nag Hammadi tractate Treatise on the Resurrection 49,9–25:

> So do not think in a partial fashion, Rheginos, nor conduct yourself in accordance with this flesh for the sake of oneness, but flee from the divisions and the bonds, and already you have the resurrection. For if one who will die knows about oneself that one will die—even if one spends many years in this life, one is brought to this—why not regard yourself as risen and brought to this?

52   "Twenty-four prophets": 2 Esdras 14:45 gives twenty-four as the number of books in the Jewish scriptures. Less relevant may be the fact that the book of Revelation and other early Christian texts give twenty-four as the number of heavenly elders.

"of you": literally, "in you."

"You have disregarded the living one . . .": Augustine, Against the Adversary of the Law and the Prophets 2.4.14, provides a close parallel to this saying: "You have rejected the living one who is before you, and you speak idly of the dead." Also noteworthy is Acts of Thomas 170: "Since you do not believe in the living, how do you wish to believe in the dead? But do not fear. Jesus the Christ, through his great goodness, treats you humanely." Compare also John 5:37–40; 8:52–53.

53   "Is circumcision useful . . .": This saying critiques the value of physical circumcision and instead recommends spiritual circumcision. Compare Romans 2:25–29, as well as other passages in Paul. According to a Jewish tradition, a governor of Judea once commented to Rabbi Akiba, "If he (that is, God) takes such pleasure in

circumcision, why then does not a child come circumcised from his mother's womb?"

54   "Fortunate are the poor . . .": Compare Matthew 5:3 (Q): Luke 6:20 (Q).

    "poor": or, "destitute" (see John Dominic Crossan, *The Historical Jesus,* pp. 270–74).

55   "Whoever does not hate . . .": Compare Matthew 10:37–38 (Q); Luke 14:26–27 (Q); Matthew 16:24; Mark 8:34; Luke 9:23; Gospel of Thomas saying 101; Manichaean Psalm Book 175,25–30: "I have left father and mother and brother and sister. I have become a stranger for the sake of your name. I have taken up my cross, and I have followed you. I have left the things of the body for the sake of the things of the spirit. I have disregarded the glory of the world for the sake of your glory that does not pass away." Note also Book of Degrees ("Liber Graduum") 3.5: "If one will not renounce all that one has and bear one's cross and follow me and imitate me, one is not worthy of me."

    "father . . . mother . . . brothers . . . sisters . . . cross": literally, "his father . . . his mother . . . his brothers . . . his sisters . . . his cross."

56   "Whoever has come to know . . .": Compare saying 80; Manichaean Kephalaia XLVIII 120,31–121,2: "The worlds that are [above] are of soul and of spirit, but [the worlds that are] below are of body and [of] carcass [. . .]. For this reason, then, he . . . the powers of heaven; he has sealed them upon their bodies and their carcasses that are in the lands. . . ." Also see saying 111.

    "carcass": in Coptic (from Greek), *ptōma.* Saying 80 has "body," *sōma.* Some scholars have suggested that "carcass" and "body" could both derive from the Aramaic word *pigra,* "corpse, body."

    "of that person the world is not worthy": This is an expression used in Jewish literature to praise someone.

57 "The father's kingdom is like . . .": the parable of the planted weeds. Compare Matthew 13:24–30. Matthew 13:36–43 consists of an allegorical interpretation of the Matthean parable.

"weeds": John Dominic Crossan, *The Historical Jesus,* pp. 279–80, cites Douglas Oakman in identifying the weed as darnel, a toxic weed that commonly infests wheat fields in the Middle East.

58 "Fortunate is the person who has worked hard": or, "Fortunate is the person who has suffered." If this is a saying about those who work hard, as is likely, mention may be made of Proverbs 8:34–36, with its commendation of a person who continually observes the ways of Wisdom, or Sirach 51:26–27, with its injunction that one labor under the yoke of Wisdom, or the Cynic author "Crates," Epistles 15 and 16, with the observation that a Cynic is one who works hard at philosophy. If this saying is about those who suffer, then compare saying 68; saying 69; James 1:12; 1 Peter 3:14a; 4:13–14; Matthew 5:10, 11 (Q); Luke 6:22 (Q).

59 "Look to the living one . . .": Compare Luke 17:22; John 7:33–36; 8:21; 13:33; Gospel of Thomas saying 38.

60 "<He saw>": This restoration parallels the structure of the opening of saying 22. It is also possible to restore saying 60 to read "<They saw>" (<*aunau*>). Either restoration assumes that the Coptic letters at the beginning of saying 60 were omitted due to haplography (that is, the inadvertent omission of something because of similar letters in the context; compare *enau* at the conclusion of saying 59 and <*afnau*> here restored at the beginning of saying 60).

"as he was going": probably the Samaritan, possibly Jesus.

"<. . .> that person <. . .> around the lamb": Literally, the Coptic text may be translated, "That person is around the lamb." It is very likely, however, that the text is corrupt, and it may possibly be restored to read something like the following: "<Why does> that person <carry> around the lamb?"

"So that he may kill it and eat it . . .": Perhaps compare Manichaean Psalm Book 172,13–27:

Necessity surrounded the love that died, the sheep that is bound [to the] tree, for which its shepherd searches. As for us [ourselves], my loved ones, let us separate the saying "Who is this that eats?" (and) "Who is this that is eaten?" —You do not (grow weary, wisdom, you do not give up, love). —[Who] is this that seeks? Who is this that is sought? The sheep that is bound to the tree, for which its shepherd searches. —You do not. — There is a sheep bound to the tree; there is another—it ate the sheep. There is a shepherd leading to pasture. He went seeking his sheep. —You do not. — The love that died is the sheep that is bound to the tree; the shepherd that seeks it is the wisdom that reveals. [The one] who ate the sheep is the consuming fire, the god of this aeon that led the entire world astray.

Within the Gospel of Thomas the themes of eating and being eaten are also found in sayings 7 and 11.

61   "Two will rest on a couch . . .": Compare Luke 17:34–35 (Q); compare and contrast Matthew 24:40–41 (Q).

"couch": or, "bed."

"Salome": Infrequently in the New Testament, and more commonly in early Christian and gnostic literature, the character Salome appears as a female follower of Jesus. In the Gospel of Thomas saying 61, she declares herself to be a follower of Jesus.

"as if you are from someone": literally, "as from one." The meaning of the Coptic is unclear. It may possibly be understood to mean "as if you are from someone special" (so Harold W. Attridge, "Greek Equivalents of Two Coptic Phrases," pp. 30–32). Bentley Layton, *Nag Hammadi Codex II,2–7*, 1.74, notes two additional possibilities: The Greek for "as a stranger" may have been mistranslated "as from one," or the Greek for "as from whom" may have been mistranslated "as from someone."

"I am the one who comes from what is whole . . .": Compare Matthew 11:27 (Q); Luke 10:22 (Q); John 3:35; 6:37–39; 13:3–4.

"whole": or, "integrated."

"<whole> . . . divided": The Coptic emended to read "<whole>" (or, "<integrated>") may be translated, without emendation, as "desolate" (*efšēf*). On the emended reading, compare Clement of Alexandria, Excerpts from Theodotus 36:1–2: "Indeed, our angels were put forth in unity, they say, being one, because they came forth from one. Now since we were divided, for this reason Jesus was baptized, that the undivided might be divided, until he unites us with them in the Fullness, so that we, the many who have become one, may all be mingled with the One that was divided for us."

"filled with light": Compare John 8:12.

62   "I disclose my mysteries . . .": Compare Matthew 13:11; Mark 4:11; Luke 8:10. In Pseudo-Clementine Homilies 19.20.1, a similar saying of Jesus is given: "Keep the mysteries for me and the sons of my house." A version of this is also found in Clement of Alexandria, Miscellanies 5.10.63.7: "My mystery is for me and the sons of my house."

"Do not let your left hand . . .": Compare Matthew 6:3.

63   "There was a rich person . . .": the parable of the rich fool. Compare Luke 12:16–21 (Q?). A similar statement about how a rich person may become overconfident and yet may die is given in Sirach 11:18–19.

"Whoever has ears . . .": This injunction to pay attention occurs throughout early Christian literature.

64   "A person was receiving guests . . .": the parable of the feast. Compare Matthew 22:1–10 (Q); Luke 14:16–24 (Q). On the excuses of the guests, compare Deuteronomy 20:5–7; 24:5. The Palestinian Talmud recounts a similar story about the rich tax-collector Bar Maʿjan, who arranged a feast for the city officials; when they did not come, he invited the poor instead.

"Buyers and merchants . . .": Sirach 26:29–27:2 also presents a statement critical of buying and selling. Sirach 26:29 reads, "Hardly will a merchant keep from wrongdoing, and a tradesman will not be acquitted of sin."

65 "A [. . .] person owned a vineyard . . .": the parable of the vineyard. The Coptic text may be restored to read either "A [good] person" (read *chrē[sto]s*) or "A creditor" (read *chrē[stē]s*; see B. Dehandschutter, "La parabole des vignerons homicides (Mc. XII,1–12) et l'évangile selon Thomas," p. 218). Compare Matthew 21:33–41; Mark 12:1–9; Luke 20:9–16.

"Perhaps he did not know them": The text may possibly be corrected to read "Perhaps <they> did not know <him>."

"Whoever has ears . . .": This injunction to pay attention occurs throughout early Christian literature.

66 "Show me the stone . . .": Compare Psalm 118:22; Matthew 21:42; Mark 12:10; Luke 20:17; Acts 4:11; 1 Peter 2:7; and other passages in early Christian literature.

67 "One who knows all but is lacking . . .": In general, compare Matthew 16:26; Mark 8:36; Luke 9:25; particularly 1 Corinthians 13:2; Book of Thomas 138,16–18: "For one who has not known oneself has not known anything, but one who has known oneself has already acquired knowledge about the depth of the universe." The saying as given in the Gospel of Thomas may presuppose the distinction, common within gnostic texts, between deficiency and fullness (of the light and spirit of God). To be filled is more important than mere knowledge.

68 "Fortunate are you when you are hated . . .": Compare Matthew 5:10, 11 (Q); Luke 6:22 (Q); Gospel of Thomas saying 58 and the note; saying 69. The parallels in Matthew and Luke (from Q) may suggest a translation employing the active voice in saying 68: "Fortunate are you when they hate you and persecute you; and they will find no place, wherever they have persecuted you." Antoine Guillaumont and the other editors of *The Gospel According to Thomas,* p. 39, propose that the Coptic text is corrupt and suggest the following understanding of the text: "you will find a place where you will

not be persecuted." Such an understanding is supported by the version of the saying in Clement of Alexandria, *Miscellanies* 4.6.41.2: "Fortunate are those who are persecuted for my sake, for they will have a place where they will not be persecuted." It is known from Eusebius that early Christians from Jerusalem attempted to escape the violence at the time of the first-century revolt against the Romans by fleeing to Pella in Transjordan. Conceivably that could be "a place where they will not be persecuted."

69   "Fortunate are those who have been persecuted . . .": Compare saying 58 and the note; saying 68 and the note. Saying 69 specifies that the place of persecution is within. In *Who Is the Rich Man?* 25, Clement of Alexandria asserts that "the most difficult persecution is from within," from pleasures and desires and passions: "The one being persecuted cannot escape it, for he carries the enemy around within himself everywhere."

      "Fortunate are they who are hungry . . .": Compare Matthew 5:6 (Q); Luke 6:21 (Q). The same juxtaposition of a commendation of the persecuted and a commendation of the hungry occurs in a letter of Mani and in Augustine.

70   "If you bring forth what is within you . . .": This saying states that salvation is achieved only when the inner, spiritual life comes to full expression. Perhaps compare saying 41 and the note on "Whoever has something"; saying 67.

71   "I shall destroy [this] house . . .": Compare Matthew 26:61; Mark 14:58; Matthew 27:40; Mark 15:29; Acts 6:14; John 2:19. In these passages Jesus (in Acts, Stephen) is said to speak of the Jewish temple; in John it is said that Jesus speaks of his bodily temple.

72   "A [person said] to him . . .": Compare Luke 12:13–14 (Q?); 'Abd al-Jabbar, *Book on the Signs of Muhammad's Prophecy*: "A man said to him, 'Master, my brother (wishes) to share (with me) my father's blessing.' (Jesus) said to him, 'Who set me over you (in order

to determine your) share?'" (in Shlomo Pines, *The Jewish Christians of the Early Centuries of Christianity According to a New Source,* p. 13). Gilles Quispel, "The *Gospel of Thomas* Revisited," p. 243, proposes that in this saying "divider" may be understood to mean "schismatic," so that Jesus denies being a schismatic or heretic. Such an understanding may be related to the Eighteen Benedictions ("Shemoneh 'Esreh") used in Jewish worship, since Benediction 12 was a prayer against Nazarenes and Minim, or heretics, and was meant to exclude such heretics (who included Jewish Christians) from the synagogue.

73–75   "Jesus said . . .": Sayings 73–75 most likely constitute a small dialogue; "He said" in saying 74 should probably be understood to mean "Someone said" (that is, someone addresses Jesus and calls him "Master").

"The harvest is large . . .": Compare Matthew 9:37–38 (Q); Luke 10:2 (Q). In Pirke Aboth 2.20, Rabbi Tarfon says, "The day is short, and the work is great, and the laborers are slow, and the wages are high, and the master of the house is insistent."

"there are many around . . .": Compare the quotation from the Heavenly Dialogue in Origen, Against Celsus 8.15: "If the son of God is stronger, and the child of humankind is his master—and who else will be master over the God who is mighty?—how is it that many are around the well and no one goes into the well? Why, when you have come to the end of so long a journey, are you lacking in daring?—You are mistaken, for I have courage and a sword."

"drinking trough": Rather than *jōte* perhaps read <*š*>*ōte*, "<well>," in the light of the citation from Origen. The Coptic word for "well" in this saying is also slightly emended (*šō*<*t*>*e* for *šōne* in the manuscript).

"nothing": or, "no one."

"There are many standing at the door . . .": Perhaps compare Matthew 25:1–13, concerning the women waiting for the bridegroom and the wedding feast.

"alone": or, "solitary." See saying 16 and the note on "alone."

76 "The father's kingdom is like a merchant . . .": the parable of the pearl. Compare Matthew 13:45–46.

"seek his treasure . . .": Compare Matthew 6:19–20 (Q); Luke 12:33 (Q); also note Matthew 13:44.

"his treasure": Perhaps read p{ef}eho, "the treasure." Antoine Guillaumont and the other editors of *The Gospel According to Thomas*, p. 42, note that the scribe initially wrote *pefho*, "his face," then added a supralinear *e*, but neglected to delete *ef*.

77 "I am the light . . .": Compare John 8:12; Manichaean Psalm Book 54,19–30:

> The strangers with whom I mingled do not know me. They tasted my sweetness and wished to keep me with them. I became life for them, but they became death for me. I bore them up, and they wore me as a garment upon them. I am in all, I bear the heavens, I am the foundation, I support the earths, I am the light that shines forth, that makes the souls rejoice. I am the life of the world, I am the milk that is in all trees, I am the sweet water that is under the children of matter.

Also compare the description of Wisdom in the Wisdom of Solomon 7:24–30.

"I am all: from me . . . to me . . .": Compare Romans 11:36; 1 Corinthians 8:6; Martyrdom of Peter 10: "You are all and all is in you. And you are what is and there is nothing else that is except you alone."

"Split a piece of wood. . . . Lift up the stone . . .": Compare Ecclesiastes 10:9; perhaps Habakkuk 2:18–20, on wooden and stone images. Note also the philosophical position presented by the Greco-Roman author Lucian of Samosata, Hermotimus 81: "God is not in heaven but rather permeates all things, such as pieces of wood and stones and animals, even the most insignificant." Papyrus Oxyrhynchus 1.23–30 combines this last part of saying 77 with a version of saying 30: "[Jesus says], 'Where there are [three, they are without] God, and where there is only [one], I say, I am with that one. Lift up the stone, and you will find me there. Split the piece of wood, and I am there.'"

78   "Why have you come out . . .": Compare Matthew 11:7–8 (Q); Luke 7:24–25 (Q).

"and your powerful ones? They are . . .": or, "and your powerful ones, who are dressed in soft clothes and cannot understand truth?"

"powerful ones": or, "members of court."

79   "Fortunate are the womb that bore you . . .": Compare Luke 11:27–28 (Q?); Petronius, Satyricon 94: "'Happy was your mother,' he said, 'who bore such a son as you; best wishes, and be good.'"

"Fortunate are those who have heard the word of the father . . .": Compare John 13:17; James 1:25.

"Fortunate are the womb that has not conceived . . .": Compare Luke 23:29; Matthew 24:19; Mark 13:17; Luke 21:23; Gospel of the Egyptians 3: "Salome says reasonably, 'Until when will people die?'. . . Therefore the master answers in a circumspect manner, 'As long as women give birth.'"

80   "Whoever has come to know . . .": Compare saying 56 and the notes.

"of that person the world is not worthy": This is an expression used in Jewish literature to praise someone.

81   "Let one who has become wealthy rule . . .": Compare 1 Corinthians 4:8; Gospel of Thomas saying 110; Dialogue of the Savior 20: "let one [who possesses] power renounce [it and repent]."

82   "Whoever is near me . . .": Nearly identical versions of this saying are quoted in Origen, in Didymus the Blind, and in an Armenian text from the Monastery of St. Lazzaro (this last text concludes with the phrase "far from life"). In Smyrnaeans 4:2 Ignatius discusses persecution and observes that "near the sword is near God; with the beasts is with God." Greek proverbs are known that parallel

saying 82 quite closely: "Whoever is near Zeus is near the thunderbolt . . . far from Zeus and the thunderbolt."

83–84 "Images are visible to people . . .": Sayings 83–84 address issues presented in Genesis 1:26–28: the creation of humankind, and the nature of the image and the likeness that characterize the human creature. These same issues are discussed in a similar fashion in Philo of Alexandria. In his Allegorical Interpretation of Genesis 1.31–32, he comments on Genesis 2:7:

> "And God formed humankind by taking clay from the earth, and he breathed into the face the breath of life, and humankind became a living soul." There are two kinds of human beings: One is heavenly, the other earthly. Now the heavenly is made in the image of God and is completely free of corruptible and earthy substance; but the earthly was constructed from matter scattered about, which he (that is, Moses) calls clay. Therefore he says that the heavenly human was not molded but was stamped in the image of God, while the earthly human is a molded thing, but not an offspring, of the Artisan. One must deduce that the human being from the earth is mind admitting but not yet being penetrated by the body.

Elsewhere, in his tractate On the Creation of the World 134, Philo describes the heavenly human, created in God's image, as "an idea or kind or seal, an object of thought, incorporeal, neither male nor female, incorruptible by nature." In the gnostic Secret Book of John II 15,2–5 the demiurge Yaldabaoth may even distinguish between the image and the likeness when he says to his authorities, "Come, let us create a human being in the image of God and in our likeness, so that the image of the human being may become a light for us." In general, compare also 2 Corinthians 3:18; 4:4–6; 1 Timothy 6:14–16.
"He will be disclosed": or, "It will be disclosed."

85 "Adam came from great power . . .": another saying interpreting Genesis 1–3. On "great power" compare Acts 8:9–10, which refers to Simon the Magician, who was said to be "the power of God that is called great." The Nag Hammadi tractate Concept of Our

Great Power also discusses the "great power," the Secret Book of John alleges that Yaldabaoth took "great power" from his mother, Wisdom, and magical texts likewise can employ the phrase "great power" to refer to a supernatural force. In the tractate On the Creation of the World 148, Philo uses the same Greek word for "power" (*dynamis*) that is used in the Coptic text of Gospel of Thomas saying 85 when he suggests that "there was probably a surpassing power about that first human."

"[he would] not [have tasted] death": On Adam tasting death, see Genesis 3:17–19.

86   "[Foxes have] their dens . . .": Compare Matthew 8:20 (Q); Luke 9:58 (Q); "Macarius" of Syria, like the Gospel of Thomas, concludes this saying with the phrase "to lay his head and rest." In Plutarch's Life of Tiberius Gracchus 9.4–5, a similar statement is made about the homeless soldiers of Italy: "The wild animals that range over Italy have a cave, and there is a lair for each of them to enter, but those who fight and die for Italy have a share in the air and the light and nothing else, but, having no house or abode, they wander about with wives and children."

"child of humankind": or, "human being"; literally, "son of man," a general reference to a person (occasionally even oneself), using a Semitic idiom.

87   "How miserable is the body . . .": Compare saying 112; saying 29; "Macarius" of Syria, Homily 1.11:

> Damn (or, Shame on) the body whenever it remains fixed in its own nature, because it becomes corrupt and dies. And damn (or, shame on) the soul if it remains fixed only in its own nature and relies only upon its own works, not having communion with the divine spirit, because it dies, not having been considered worthy of the eternal life of divinity.

Saying 87 observes that a person who bases his or her welfare—body and soul—upon the bodily world will be disappointed. The words "these two" probably refer to the two bodies mentioned in the first part of the saying.

88 "The messengers and the prophets will come to you . . .": This saying may discuss interactions with itinerant prophets or with heavenly messengers. The word *angelos* used in the Coptic may be translated either "messengers" or "angels." In the Jewish scriptures and the New Testament, this word may designate either sort of messenger; at times it may indicate a prophet or a human emissary. In the Discourses of Epictetus a Cynic philosopher may be called a "messenger" of Zeus to humankind.

"give you what is yours. You, in turn, give them what you have . . .": Perhaps compare saying 21 (the owners of the world reclaim the fleshly garments); Secret Book of John II 25,33–26,7 (those who receive the body eventually meet the soul); Authoritative Teaching 32,16–33,3 (the dealers in bodies do business with bodies and souls). Conversely, Gospel of Thomas saying 88 may simply describe interactions with prophets and teachers.

89 "Why do you wash . . .": Compare Matthew 23:25–26 (Q); Luke 11:39–41 (Q). Note also the Babylonian Talmud, Berakoth 51a, with its provisions for rinsing the inside and washing the outside of a cup; also Kelim 25.1–9, with its discussion of laws concerning the inner and outer sides of various vessels.

90 "Come to me, for my yoke is easy . . .": Compare Matthew 11:28–30. Also compare the saying of Wisdom in Sirach 51:26–27: "Put your neck under the yoke, and let your soul receive instruction; it is nearby to find. See with your eyes that I have labored little and have found for myself much rest."

"rest": See saying 2 and the note.

91 "Tell us who you are . . .": Compare Matthew 16:1, 2–3 (Q); Luke 12:54–56 (Q).

92   "Seek and you will find": Compare saying 94; saying 2 and the note; Matthew 7:7–8 (Q); Luke 11:9–10 (Q).

"In the past, however, I did not tell you . . .": Compare John 16:4–5, 12–15, 22–28.

93   "Do not give what is holy . . .": Compare Matthew 7:6; the saying is also quoted in the Didache, Tertullian, Hippolytus, Epiphanius, and the Book of Degrees.

"or they might . . . it [. . .]": Several possible restorations of this passage have been suggested, but none has proven to be convincing. Bentley Layton, *Nag Hammadi Codex II,2–7,* 1.86–87, notes the following suggestions: "or they might make [mud] of it"; "or they might bring it [to naught]"; "or they might grind it [to bits]."

94   "One who seeks will find . . .": Compare saying 92; saying 2 and the note; Matthew 7:7–8 (Q); Luke 11:9–10 (Q).

95   "If you have money . . .": Compare Matthew 5:42 (Q); Luke 6:30 (Q), 34–35b (Q?), 35c (Q); Didache 1:5: "Give to everyone who asks of you, and do not ask for it back, for the father wishes that to all should be given of his own gifts." In the present saying we might expect to read [*emmoou*] (or the like) rather than [*emmof*].

96   "The father's kingdom is like [a] woman . . .": the parable of the leaven. Compare Matthew 13:33 (Q); Luke 13:20–21 (Q).

"Whoever has ears . . ." This injunction to pay attention occurs throughout early Christian literature.

97   "The [father's] kingdom is like a woman who was carrying a [jar] full of meal . . .": the parable of the jar of meal. This parable is known only here in early Christian literature, although "Macarius" of Syria tells a somewhat similar story of a bag full of sand that is leaking out through a tiny hole in the bag.

"walking along [a] distant road": or, "walking along [the] road, still far off" (restoring to read *h[i te]hie*).

"she had not noticed a problem": or, "she had not understood how to toil" (so Bentley Layton, *The Gnostic Scriptures,* p. 396).

98   "The father's kingdom is like a person . . .": the parable of the assassin. This parable, too, is known only here in early Christian literature. In general, compare saying 35; Matthew 11:12–13 (Q); Luke 16:16 (Q).
   "someone powerful": or, "a member of court."
   "go in": or, "be strong enough."
   "powerful one": or, "member of court."

99   "The followers said to him, 'Your brothers and your mother . . .' ": Compare Matthew 12:46–50; Mark 3:31–35; Luke 8:19–21; Gospel of the Ebionites 5:

> Furthermore, they (that is, the Ebionites) deny that he (that is, Christ) was a human being, apparently from the saying that the savior spoke when it was reported to him, "Look, your mother and your brothers are standing outside": "Who are my mother and brothers?" And extending his hand toward the followers, he said, "These are my brothers and mother and sisters, who do the will of my father."

2 Clement 9:11 also gives the saying, "My brothers are these who do the will of my father."

100   "They showed Jesus a gold coin . . .": Compare Matthew 22:15–22; Mark 12:13–17; Luke 20:20–26; Papyrus Egerton 2 2r,43–59 tells a more general story with some of the same features. Note also Sentences of Sextus 20: "Give precisely the things of the world to the world and the things of God to God." The command "give me what is mine," found only in the Gospel of Thomas, elevates the place of Jesus.

101   "Whoever does not hate . . .": Compare Matthew 10:37–38 (Q); Luke 14:26–27 (Q); Gospel of Thomas saying 55.

"[father] and mother": literally, "his [father] and his mother."

"[father and] mother": literally, "his [father and] his mother."

"For my mother [. . .]": The text cannot be restored with confidence. One possibility: "For my mother [gave me falsehood]" (restoring to read *entaṣ[ti naei empc]ol;* see Bentley Layton, *Nag Hammadi Codex II,2–7*, 1.88).

"my true [mother]": perhaps the holy spirit, who may be described as the mother of Jesus in such texts as the Secret Book of James, the Gospel of the Hebrews, and the Gospel of Philip. Thus the conundrum presented in the saying (hate parents and love parents) is resolved by positing two orders of family and two mothers of Jesus.

102   "Damn the Pharisees . . .": or, "Shame on the Pharisees. . . ." Compare similar statements in Matthew 23:13 (Q); Luke 11:52 (Q); see also Gospel of Thomas saying 39.

"they are like a dog sleeping in the cattle manger . . .": This is a well-known theme in folk literature, and parallels occur in Aesop and Lucian. Compare, for example, Aesop, Fable 702: "A wicked dog was lying in a manger that was full of hay. When the cattle came to eat, it would not let them but bared its teeth in a threatening expression. The cattle then said to it, 'It is unfair for you to begrudge us the natural appetite that you do not have. For it is not your nature to eat hay, and yet you prevent us from eating it.'"

103   "Fortunate is the person who knows where the robbers . . .": Compare saying 21; Matthew 24:43 (Q); Luke 12:39 (Q).

104   "They said to Jesus, 'Come, let us pray today and let us fast' . . .": Compare Matthew 9:14–15; Mark 2:18–20; Luke 5:33–35; also Gospel of the Nazoreans 2: "Look, the mother of the master and his brothers said to him, 'John the Baptist is baptizing for the remission of sins. Let us go and be baptized by him.' But he said to them, 'What sin have I committed, that I should hasten and be baptized by him? Unless perchance this very thing that I have said is ignorance.'"

For similar critiques of Jewish or Jewish-Christian observance in the Gospel of Thomas, see sayings 6; 14; 53.

105 "Whoever knows the father and the mother . . .": This saying may be interpreted as a recommendation that one despise one's physical parents; compare sayings 55; 101. Book of Thomas 144,8–10 declares, "Damn you who love intercourse and filthy association with womankind." In Irenaeus, Against Heresies 1.23.2, evidence may be provided for another interpretation of the saying. There Irenaeus explains that Simon the Magician's associate Helena, a prostitute from Tyre, was understood to be the divine thought that was incarnated in body after body and that even became a whore, though she is actually "the mother of all." In a similar vein, the myth of the soul as presented in the Nag Hammadi text Exegesis on the Soul explains how the soul is raped and abused in the body and how the soul falls into prostitution. Origen may give reason to consider yet another interpretation of the saying. In Against Celsus 1.28; 32 Origen cites the tradition that Jesus was the illegitimate child of Mary, who "bore a child from a certain soldier named Panthera." It is known from a gravestone that a Sidonian archer named Tiberius Julius Abdes Pantera was in fact stationed in Palestine around the time of the birth of Jesus. In this regard perhaps compare John 8:41.

106 "When you make the two into one . . .": On this saying in general, see saying 48 and the note. On making two into one, see saying 4 and the note on becoming one.

107 "The kingdom is like a shepherd . . .": the parable of the lost sheep. Compare Matthew 18:12–13 (Q); Luke 15:4–7 (Q); also note Ezekiel 34:15–16. In the Babylonian Talmud, a contrast is made between ninety-nine people who urge one thing and one person who is more on the side of the law; and in the Midrash Rabbah of Genesis, a person is described leaving eleven cows to find the one that wandered away.

108 "Whoever drinks from my mouth . . .": Compare saying 13; John 4:13–14; 7:37–39; 1 Corinthians 10:1–4; Sirach 24:21, on drinking of Wisdom. In Odes of Solomon 30:1, 5, it is said that living water flows from the lips of the Lord.

"I myself shall become that person": What is promised is a mystical identification of Jesus with the follower of Jesus.

"the hidden things . . .": Compare sayings 5 and 6 and the note on what is hidden.

109 "The kingdom is like a person . . .": the parable of the treasure. On wisdom as a hidden treasure, compare Proverbs 2:1–5; Sirach 20:30–31. In addition to Matthew 13:44, sources such as the Midrash Rabbah and Aesop contain stories with parallels to saying 109:

> Rabbi Simeon ben Yohai taught, "It is like a person who inherited some land that was a manure pile. Now the heir was lazy, and he went and sold it at a very low price. The buyer went to work and dug in it, and in it he found a treasure, and from that he built a great palace. The buyer began going around in public with servants following behind, from the treasure he got in it. Seeing this, the seller was ready to choke and said, 'Ah, what have I lost!'" (Midrash Rabbah, Song of Songs 4.12.1)

> A farmer who was about to die and who wished to familiarize his sons with farming summoned them and said, "Sons, in one of my vineyards a treasure is hidden." After his death they took plows and mattocks and dug up all of their farmed land. They did not find the treasure, but the vineyard repaid them with a harvest many times greater. The story shows that what is gotten from toil is a treasure for people. (Aesop, Fable 42)

110 "Let someone who has found the world . . .": Compare saying 81. The teaching on renunciation of the world also occurs in the Acts of Paul and Thecla, the Acts of Peter and the Twelve Apostles, and Pistis Sophia. See also Gospel of Thomas saying 27 on fasting from (or, abstaining from) the world.

111 "The heavens and the earth will roll up . . .": Several Jewish and early Christian documents describe the heavens being rolled up like a scroll: Isaiah 34:4; Psalm 102:25–27 (some ancient texts); Hebrews 1:10–12; Revelation 6:13–14.

"whoever is living from the living one . . .": Compare John 11:25–26.

"Does not Jesus say . . .": This is a separate saying, but the unusual quotation formula that introduces it may suggest that this is a later comment incorporated into the saying. Compare sayings 56 and 80.

"of that person the world is not worthy": This is an expression used in Jewish literature to praise someone.

112 "Damn the flesh . . . Damn the soul . . .": or, "Shame on the flesh . . . Shame on the soul. . . ." Compare saying 87; saying 29; "Macarius" of Syria, Homily 1.11 (cited at saying 87).

113 "It will not come by watching for it . . .": Compare Mark 13:21–23; Matthew 24:23–25, 26–27 (Q); Luke 17:20–22, 23–24 (Q); Gospel of Thomas saying 3; Gospel of Mary 8,11–22: "When the blessed one had said these things, he greeted them all, saying, 'Peace be with you. Acquire my peace for yourselves. Watch that no one mislead you, saying, "Look, here," or, "Look, there," for the child of humankind is within you. Follow him. Those who seek him will find him. Go, then, and preach the gospel of the kingdom.'"

"It will not be said": or, "They will not say" (compare Luke 17:20–21).

"the father's kingdom is spread out upon the earth . . .": "Macarius" of Syria preserves a nearly identical saying of Jesus: "God's kingdom is spread out upon the earth, and people do not see it." See Gilles Quispel, "The Syrian Thomas and the Syrian Macarius," p. 113. Similarly, in Jewish literature, Sirach 1:9 states that the Lord "poured her (that is, Wisdom) out upon all his works," and Testament of Levi 18:5 declares that in the days to come "the knowledge of the Lord will be poured out upon the earth like the water of the seas."

114   "Simon Peter said to them, 'Mary should leave us . . .'": In gnostic literature Peter sometimes opposes Mary with hostile and sexist sentiments.

"every female who makes herself male . . .": The transformation of the female into the male is discussed extensively in ancient literature (the transformation of the male into the female is also discussed, in the context of the acts of self-castration within the mysteries of the Great Mother and Attis). A few ancient accounts, in authors like Ovid and Phlegon of Tralles, communicate fantastic stories of women sprouting male genitals and thus becoming male, but most of the accounts use the gender categories in a metaphorical sense. Often the transformation of the female into the male involves the transformation of all that is earthly, perishable, passive, and sense-perceptible into what is heavenly, imperishable, active, and rational. In short, what is connected with the earth Mother is to be transformed into what is connected with the sky Father. If this is a correct interpretation of Gospel of Thomas saying 114, then the saying is intended to be a statement of liberation, although the specific use of gender categories may be shocking to modern sensitivities. Compare these quotations from Hippolytus, Clement of Alexandria, the First Apocalypse of James, and Zostrianos:

> For this, he says, is "the gate of heaven," . . . where it is necessary for them, when they have come there, to cast off their clothing and all become bridegrooms, having been made male through the virgin spirit. (Hippolytus, Refutation of All Heresies 5.8.44)

> As long, then, as the seed is still unformed, they say, it is a child of the female, but when it was formed, it was changed into a man and becomes a son of the bridegroom. No longer is it weak and subject to the cosmic (forces), visible and invisible, but, having become male, it becomes a male fruit. (Clement of Alexandria, Excerpts from Theodotus 79)

The perishable has gone [up] to the imperishable, and [the] element of femaleness has attained to the element of this maleness. (First Apocalypse of James 41,15–19)

Do not baptize yourselves with death, nor give yourselves into the hands of those who are inferior to you instead of those who are better. Flee from the madness and the bondage of femaleness, and choose for yourselves the salvation of maleness. You have not come [to] suffer, but rather you have come to escape your bondage. (Zostrianos 131,2–10)

It is suggested in these quotations that all people on the earth, whether women or men, must undergo this change. For a similar statement of transformation that is also meant to be liberating but that uses gender categories very differently, see Gospel of Thomas saying 22. For a full discussion of saying 114, see Marvin W. Meyer, "Making Mary Male: The Categories 'Male' and 'Female' in the Gospel of Thomas."

"Whoever discovers the interpretation of these sayings . . ."

A READING

by HAROLD BLOOM

The popularity of the Gospel of Thomas among Americans is another indication that there is indeed "the American religion": creedless, Orphic, enthusiastic, proto-gnostic, post-Christian. Unlike the canonical gospels, that of Judas Thomas the Twin spares us the crucifixion, makes the resurrection unnecessary, and does not present us with a God named Jesus. No dogmas could be founded upon this sequence (if it is a sequence) of apothegms. If you turn to the Gospel of Thomas, you encounter a Jesus who is unsponsored and free. No one could be burned or even scorned in the name of this Jesus, and no one has been hurt in any way, except perhaps for those bigots, high church or low, who may have glanced at so permanently surprising a work.

I take it that the first saying is not by Jesus but by his twin, who states the interpretive challenge and its prize: more life into a time without boundaries. That was and is the blessing: "The kingdom is inside you and it is outside you." Marvin Meyer is wary when it comes to naming these hidden sayings as gnostic, but I will not hesitate in making this brief commentary into a gnostic sermon that takes the Gospel of Thomas for its text. What makes us free is the *gnōsis,* and the hidden sayings set down by Thomas form a part of a *gnōsis* available to every Christian, Jew, humanist, skeptic, whoever you are. The trouble of finding, and being found, is simply the trouble that clears ignorance away, to be replaced by the gnostic knowing in which we are known even as we know ourselves. The alternative is precisely what Emerson and Wallace Stevens meant by "poverty": imaginative lack or need. To believe that anything whatsoever *is* so does not redress "poverty" in this sense. Knowledge only is the remedy, and such knowledge must be knowledge of the self. The Jesus of the Gospel of Thomas calls us to knowledge and not to belief, for faith need not lead to wisdom; and this Jesus is a wisdom teacher, gnomic and wandering, rather than a proclaimer of finalities. You cannot be a minister of this gospel, nor found a church upon it. The Jesus who urges his followers to be passersby is a remarkably Whitmanian Jesus, and there is little in the Gospel of Thomas that would not have been accepted by Emerson, Thoreau, and Whitman.

Seeing what is before you is the whole art of vision for Thomas's Jesus. Many of the hidden sayings are so purely antithetical that they can be interpreted only by our seeing what they severely decline to affirm. No scholar ever will define precisely what gnosticism was or is, but its negations are palpable. Nothing mediates the self for the Jesus of the Gospel of Thomas. Everything we seek is already in our presence, and not outside our self. What is most remarkable in these sayings is the repeated insistence that everything is already open to you. You need but knock and enter. What is best and oldest in you will respond fully to what you allow yourself to see. The deepest teaching of this gnostic Jesus is never stated but always implied, implied in nearly every saying. There is light in you, and that light is no part of the created world. It is not Adamic. I know of only two convictions essential to the *gnōsis:* Creation and fall were one and the same event; and what is best in us was never created, so cannot fall. The American religion, *gnōsis* of our Evening-Land, adds a third element if our freedom is to be complete. That ultimate spark of the pre-created light must be alone, or at least alone with Jesus. The living Jesus of the Gospel of Thomas speaks to all the followers, but in the crucial thirteenth saying he speaks to Thomas alone, and those secret three sayings are never revealed to us. Here we must surmise, since those three solitary sayings are the hidden heart of the Gospel of Thomas.

Thomas has earned knowledge of the sayings (or words) by denying any similitude for Jesus. His twin is not like a just messenger or prophet, nor is he like a wise philosopher, or teacher of Greek wisdom. The sayings then would turn upon the nature of Jesus: what he is. He is so much of the light as to be the light, but not the light of heaven, or of the heaven above heaven. The identification must be with the stranger or alien God, not the God of Moses and of Adam, but the man-god of the abyss, prior to creation. Yet that is only one truth out of three, though quite enough to be stoned for, and then avenged by divine fire. The second saying must be the call of that stranger God to Thomas, and the third must be the response of Thomas, which is his realization that he already is in the place of rest, alone with his twin.

Scholars increasingly assert that certain sayings in the Gospel of Thomas are closer to the hypothetical "Q" document than are parallel passages in the synoptic gospels. They generally ascribe the gnostic overtones of the Gospel of Thomas to a redactor, perhaps a Syrian ascetic of the second century of the Common Era. I would advance a different hypothesis, though with little expectation that scholars would welcome it. Of the veritable text of the sayings of a historical Jesus, we have nothing. Presumably he spoke to his followers and other wayfarers in Aramaic, and except for a few phrases scattered through the gospels, none of his Aramaic sayings has survived. I have wondered for some time how this could be, and wondered even more that Christian scholars have never joined in my wonder. If you believed in the divinity of Jesus, would you not wish to have preserved the actual Aramaic sentences he spoke, since they were for you the words of God? But what was preserved were Greek translations of his sayings, rather than the Aramaic sayings themselves. Were they lost, still to be found in a cave somewhere in Israel? Were they never written down in the first place, so that the Greek texts were based only upon memory? For some years now, I have asked these questions whenever I have met a New Testament scholar, and I have met only blankness. Yet surely this puzzle matters. Aramaic and Greek are very different languages, and the nuances of spirituality and of wisdom do not translate readily from one into the other. Any sayings of Jesus, open or hidden, need to be regarded in this context, which ought to teach us a certain suspicion of even the most normative judgments as to authenticity, whether those judgments rise from faith or from supposedly positive scholarship.

My skepticism is preamble to my hypothesis that the gnostic sayings that crowd the Gospel of Thomas indeed may come from Q, or from some *ur*-Q, which would mean that there were protognostic elements in the teachings of Jesus. The Gospel of Mark, in my reading, is far closer to the J-writer or Yahwist than are the other gospels; and while I hardly find any gnostic shadings in Mark or the Yahwist, I do find uncanny moments not reconcilable with official Christianity and Judaism. Moshe Idel, the great revisionist scholar of Kabbalah, persuades me that what seem gnostic elements in Kabbalah actually stem from an archaic Jewish religion, anything but normative, of which what we call gnosticism may be an echo or parody. Christian gnosticism also may be a belated version of some of the teachings of Jesus. All of gnosticism, according to the late Ioan Couliano, is a kind of creative misinterpretation or strong misreading or misprision both of Plato and the Bible. Sometimes, as I contemplate organized, institutional Christianity, historical and contemporary, it seems to me a very weak misreading of the teachings of Jesus. The Gospel of Thomas speaks to me, and to many others, Gentile and Jewish, in ways that Matthew, Luke, and John certainly do not.

This excursus returns me to my professedly gnostic sermon upon the text of the Gospel of Thomas. How do the secret sayings of Jesus help to make us free? What knowledge do they give us of who we were, of what we have become, of where we were, of wherein we have been thrown, of whereto we are hastening, of what we are being freed, of what birth really is, of what rebirth really is? A wayfaring Jesus, as presented in Burton Mack's *A Myth of Innocence,* is accepted by Marvin Meyer as his vision of the Jesus of the Gospel of Thomas, an acceptance in which I am happy to share. Mack rightly emphasizes that every text we have of Jesus is late; I would go a touch further and call them anxiously "belated." Indeed, I return to my earlier question about our lack of the Aramaic text of what Jesus said: Is it not an extraordinary scandal that *all* the crucial texts of Christianity are so surprisingly belated? The Gospel of Mark is at least forty years later than the passion that supposedly it records, and the hypothetical Q depends upon collating materials from Matthew and Luke, perhaps seventy years after the event. Mack's honest and sensible conclusion is to postulate a Jesus whose career does not center upon crucifixion and resurrection, but upon the wanderings of a kind of Cynic sage. Such a sage, in my own reading of the Gospel of Thomas, may well have found his way back to an earlier version of the Jewish religion than any we now recognize. And that earliness, as Idel has shown, anticipated much of what we now call gnosticism.

What begins to make us free is the *gnōsis* of who we were, when we were "in the light." When we were in the light, then we stood at the beginning, immovable, fully human, and so also divine. To know who we were, is to be known as we now wish to be known. We came into being before coming into being; we already were, and so never were created. And yet what we have become altogether belies that origin that was already an end. The Jesus of the Gospel of Thomas refrains from saying precisely how dark we have become, but subtly he indicates perpetually what we now are. We dwell in poverty, and we *are* that poverty, for our imaginative need has become greater than our imaginations can fulfill. The emphasis of this Jesus is upon a pervasive opacity that prevents us from seeing anything that really matters. Ignorance is the blocking agent that thwarts the ever-early Jesus, and his implied interpretation of our ignorance is: belatedness. The hidden refrain of these secret or dark sayings is that we are blinded by an overwhelming sense that we have come after the event, indeed, after ourselves. What the gnostic Jesus warns against is retroactive meaningfulness, repetitive and incessant aftering. He has not come to praise famous men, and our fathers who were before us. Of men, he commends only John the Baptist and his own brother, James the Just. The normative nostalgia for the virtues of the fathers is totally absent. Present all around us and yet evading us are the intimations of the light, unseen except by Jesus.

An admonition against retroactive meaningfulness is neither Platonic nor normatively Jewish, and perhaps hints again at an archaic Jewish spirituality, of which apparent gnosticism may be the shadow. The gnostic hatred of time is implicit in the Gospel of Thomas. Is it only a vengeful misprision both of Plato and the Hebrew Bible, or does it again hint at an archaic immediacy that Jesus, as wandering teacher, seeks to revive? Moshe Idel finds in some of the most ancient extra-biblical texts the image we associate now with Hermeticism and Kabbalah, the primordial Human, whom the angels resented and envied. To pass from that Anthropos to Adam is to fall into time, by a fall that is only the creation of Adam and his world. Certainly the Jesus of the Gospel of Thomas has no fondness for Adam, who "came from great power and great wealth, but he was not worthy of you."

Where were we, then, before we were Adam? In a place before creation, but not a world elsewhere. The kingdom, which we do not see, nevertheless is spread out upon the earth. Normative Judaism, from its inception, spoke of hallowing the commonplace, but the Jesus of the Gospel of Thomas beholds nothing that is commonplace. Since the kingdom is inside us and outside us, what is required is that we bring the axis of vision and the axis of things together again. The stones themselves will then serve us, transparent to our awakened vision. Though the Gospel of Thomas avoids using the gnostic terms for the fullness, the Pleroma, and the cosmological emptiness, the Kenoma, their equivalents hover in the discourse of the wandering teacher of open vision. The living Jesus, never the man who was crucified nor the god who was resurrected, is himself the fullness of where once we were. And that surely is one of the effects of the Gospel of Thomas, which is to undo the Jesus of the New Testament and return us to an earlier Jesus. Burton Mack's central argument seems to me unassailable: The Jesus of the churches is founded upon the literary character, Jesus, as composed by Mark. I find this parallel to my argument, in *The Book of J,* that the Western worship of God—Judaic, Christian, Islamic—is the worship not only of a literary character, but of the wrong literary character, the God of Ezra the Redactor rather than the uncanny Yahweh of the J writer. If the Jesus of the Gospel of Thomas is also to be regarded as a literary character, then at least he too will be the right literary character, like the Davidic-Solomonic Yahweh.

Wherein, according to Thomas's Jesus, have we been thrown? Into the body, the world, and our temporal span in this world, or in the sum: Have we been thrown into everything that is not ourselves? I would not interpret this as a call to ascetic renunciation, since other sayings in the Gospel of Thomas reject fasting, almsgiving, and all particular diets. And though the Jesus of Thomas is hardly a libertine gnostic, his call to end both maleness and femaleness does not read to me as an evasion of all sexuality. We are not told what will make the two into one, and we should interpret this conversion into one composite gender as something beyond the absorption of the female into the male. Everything here turns upon the image of the entrance of the bridegroom into the wedding chamber, which can be accomplished only by those who are solitaries, elitist individuals who in some sense have transcended gender distinctions. But this solitude need not be an ascetic condition, and it repeats or rejoins the figure of the pre-Adamic Anthropos, the human before the fall-into-creation. That figure, whether in ancient Jewish speculation (as Idel shows), or in gnosticism, or in Kabbalah, is hardly removed from sexual experience.

Whereto are we hastening? Few of the hidden sayings of Jesus suggest that the destination of most of us is a solitary entrance into the wedding chamber. Whatever gnosticism was, or is, it must clearly be an elitist phenomenon, an affair of intellectuals, or of mystical intellectuals. The Gospel of Thomas addresses itself only to a subtle elite, those capable of knowing, who then through knowing can come to see what Jesus insists is plainly visible before them, indeed all around them. This Jesus has not come to take away the sins of the world, or to atone for all humankind. As one who passes by, he urges his seekers to learn to be passersby, to cease hastening to the temporal death of business and busyness that the world miscalls life. It is the busy world of death-in-life that constitutes the whatness from which we are being freed by the Jesus of the Gospel of Thomas. There is no haste in this Jesus, no apocalyptic intensity. He does not teach the end-time, but rather a transvaluation of time, in the here of our moment.

What really is birth? The peculiar emphasis of the question, in this context, is authentically gnostic, and reverberates throughout the hidden sayings of Jesus. Here the transcendental bitterness of logion 79 is wholly appropriate:

> A woman in the crowd said to him, "Fortunate are the womb that bore you and the breasts that fed you."
> He said to [her], "Fortunate are those who have heard the word of the father and have truly kept it. For there will be days when you will say, 'Fortunate are the womb that has not conceived and the breasts that have not given milk.' "

This relates to the enigmatic saying 101, where the "true" mother evidently is distinguished from the natural or actual mother, and to the strikingly antithetical 105:

> Jesus said, "Whoever knows the father and the mother will be called the child of a whore."

The crux there is "know," since only the original self or spark should be known, instead of one's natural descent. Like many other wisdom teachers, this Jesus practices a rhetoric of shock in order to break down preconceived associations. His onslaught upon one's own mother and father implicitly justifies its violence by questioning not so much motherhood or fatherhood, but birth itself. Even the natural birth of Jesus still participates in the creation-fall, still resists rebirth in the spirit and in a father, whose fatherhood is only a metaphor for a dwelling together.

I have been founding this sermon-as-commentary upon a famous Valentinian gnostic formula, and the Gospel of Thomas has no specific sayings that are Valentinian as such. But the Valentinian chant has features so broad that by it we can chart most other varieties of gnostic religion. Its culminating and crucial question asks what rebirth really is, and many of the hidden sayings of Jesus turn ultimately upon answering that question. Rebirth involves joining Thomas as a sharer in the solitude of Jesus, or being a passerby with Jesus. In the United States, this hardly requires commentary, since it is the situation of the Baptist walking alone with Jesus, whether he or she be black Baptist or moderate Southern Baptist or independent. The American Jesus, from the nineteenth century through now, is far closer to the wanderer of the Gospel of Thomas than to the crucified Jesus of the New Testament. The "living Jesus" of Thomas has been resurrected without the need of having first been sacrificed, which is the paradox also of the American Jesus.

My gnostic sermon has concluded; the coda is a post-sermon reflection upon the allied strangenesses of gnosticism, and of Christianity in any of its varieties, permutations even more bewildering than those of what Hans Jonas taught us to call the gnostic religion. Between Jesus and any Christianity, at least a generation of silence intervenes. There is a grand, almost tragic absurdity in attempting to translate that text back into Aramaic. Nietzsche, himself a master of aphorism, insisted that an exclusive writing or teaching by aphorism was a decadent mode. Kafka, this century's master of aphorism, turned to it as the most desperately appropriate of literary modes. Long a kind of Jewish gnostic, I remember still my unhappy aesthetic shock at first reading translations of the Nag Hammadi texts. The fragments quoted by the heresiologists, particularly the magnificent fragments of Valentinus, far surpassed any of the newly discovered texts, with the single exception of the Valentinian Gospel of Truth. It is the sorrow of ancient gnosticism that, except for Valentinus, it produced no author worthy of its imaginative energies. Jesus, whoever he was and whatever he was, appears in Q and in the Gospel of Thomas as a great verbal artist in the oral tradition. That was Oscar Wilde's vision of Jesus, and G. Wilson Knight's, following Wilde, and I prefer Wilde and Wilson Knight on Jesus to all of the New

Testament scholars, who are not exactly out to ruin the sacred truths. Sacred truths have a way of turning out to be either bad literary criticism or else coercion, whether open or concealed.

But the Jesus of the Gospel of Thomas is not interested in coercion, nor can anyone coerce in his name. The innocence of gnosticism is its freedom from violence and fraud, from which historical Christianity cannot be disentangled. No one is going to establish a gnostic church in America, by which I mean a professedly gnostic church, to which tax exemption would never be granted anyway. Of course we have gnostic churches in plenty: the Mormons, the Southern Baptists, the Assemblies of God, Christian Science, and most other indigenous American denominations and sects. These varieties of the American religion, as I call it, are all involuntary parodies of the *gnōsis* of the Gospel of Thomas. But ancient gnosticism is neither to be praised nor blamed for its modern analogues. What is surely peculiar is the modern habit of employing "gnosis" or "gnosticism" as a conservative or institutionalized Christian term of abuse. An elitist religion, gnosticism almost always has been a severely intellectual phenomenon, and the Jesus of the Gospel of Thomas is certainly the most intellectualized figure among all the versions of Jesus through the ages. The appeal of this Jesus is not to the mind alone, and yet his rhetoric demands a considerable effort of cognition if it is to be unpacked:

> Fortunate is the lion that the human will eat, so that the lion becomes human. And foul is the human that the lion will eat, and the lion will become human.

Perhaps there is a recondite reference here to the gnostic figure of the demiurgical false creator, sometimes depicted as a lion, but the imaginative strength of this apothegm does not depend on an esoteric mythology. Whether or not you judge the Gospel of Thomas to be gnostic in its orientation, you are confronted here by what I would suggest is an ancient humanism, one that is difficult to reconcile either with late Judaism or early Christianity. This hard saying of Jesus opposes two ways of becoming human, one blessed and the other foul. If we devour the lion in us, we are blessed, and if the lion feasts on the knowing part of us, then we are lost. For the kingly lion in us knows nothing except its projection outward of its own being as lord of creation, but what is most human in us is no part of creation. And there is the center of the aphorisms that make up the Gospel of Thomas, a center that goes back to the origin, to the fullness of the abyss that preceded creation. There too, as I interpret it, is the last negation of the Gospel of Thomas, which we wrong by interpreting merely as an exhortation to asceticism:

> Simon Peter said to them, "Mary should leave us, for females are not worthy of life."
>
> Jesus said, "Look, I shall guide her to make her male, so that she too may become a living spirit resembling you males. For every female who makes herself male will enter heaven's kingdom."

This violently figurative language can be weakly misread as the ascetic's revulsion from nature or the female, a misreading particularly troublesome at our time, in our place, as it were. But "life" or "living" here means what it does in "the living Jesus" of the prologue to the Gospel of Thomas. That "living" Jesus certainly is not male in the literal but in a metaphorical sense, the metaphor belonging to the gnostic sense of the original abyss, at once our forefather and our foremother. Whatever surges beneath the surface of the Gospel of Thomas, it is not a Syrian Christian wisdom teaching of the second century. The ascetic accepts creation, but always upon the basis of having fallen from it, and always with the hope of being restored to it. That is hardly the aspiration of Jesus in the Gospel of Thomas. Like William Blake, like Jakob Böhme, this Jesus is looking for the face he had before the world was made. That marvelous trope I appropriate from W. B. Yeats, at his most Blakean. If such is your quest, then the Gospel of Thomas calls out to you.

BIBLIOGRAPHY

Attridge, Harold W. "Greek Equivalents of Two Coptic Phrases: CG
    I,1. 65,9–10 and CG II,2. 43.26." *Bulletin of the American
    Society of Papyrologists* 18 (1981): 27–32.
———. "The Original Text of Gos. Thom., Saying 30." *Bulletin of
    the American Society of Papyrologists* 16 (1979): 153–57.
Baarda, Tjitze. "Jesus Said: Be Passers-By: On the Meaning and
    Origin of Logion 42 of the Gospel of Thomas." Pp.
    179–205 in idem, *Early Transmission of Words of Jesus:
    Thomas, Tatian and the Text of the New Testament*. Ed.
    J. Helderman and S. J. Noorda. Amsterdam: VU
    Boekhandel/Uitgeverij, 1983.
Baker, Aelred. "'Fasting to the World.'" *Journal of Biblical Literature*
    84 (1965): 291–94.
———. "Pseudo-Macarius and the Gospel of Thomas." *Vigiliae
    Christianae* 18 (1964): 215–25.
Bauer, Johannes B. "Das Jesuswort 'Wer mir nahe ist.' " *Theologische
    Zeitschrift* 15 (1959): 446–50.
Biblical Archeologist 42 (1979): 194–256: Fall issue devoted to the Nag
    Hammadi story.
Bloom, Harold. *The American Religion: The Emergence of the Post-
    Christian Nation*. New York: Simon and Schuster, 1992.
Brown, Raymond E. "The Gospel of Thomas and St John's
    Gospel." *New Testament Studies* 9 (1962–63): 155–77.
Cameron, Ron. "Parable and Interpretation in the Gospel of
    Thomas." *Foundations and Facets Forum* 2 (1986): 3–39.
———. "Thomas, Gospel of." Pp. 535–40 in vol. 6 of *The Anchor
    Bible Dictionary*. Ed. David Noel Freedman. Garden City,
    NY: Doubleday, 1992.
Crossan, John Dominic. *The Historical Jesus: The Life of a
    Mediterranean Jewish Peasant*. San Francisco: Harper San
    Francisco, 1991.

Dart, John. *The Jesus of Heresy and History: The Discovery and Meaning of the Nag Hammadi Gnostic Library*. San Francisco: Harper & Row, 1988.

Davies, Stevan L. *The Gospel of Thomas and Christian Wisdom*. New York: Seabury, 1983.

De Conick, April D., and Jarl Fossum. "Stripped Before God: A New Interpretation of Logion 37 in the *Gospel of Thomas*." *Vigiliae Christianae* 45 (1991): 123–50.

Dehandschutter, B. "La parabole des vignerons homicides (Mc. XII, 1–12) et l'évangile selon Thomas." Pp. 203–19 in *L'évangile selon Marc: Tradition et rédaction*. Ed. M. Sabbe. Bibliotheca ephemeridum theologicarum lovaniensium 34. Gembloux: Louvain University Press/Duculot, 1974.

Döllinger, Ignaz von. *Beiträge zur Sektengeschichte des Mittelalters*. 2 vols. München: Beck; Darmstadt: Wissenschaftliche Buchgesellschaft, 1968.

Evelyn-White, Hugh G. *The Sayings of Jesus from Oxyrhynchus*. Cambridge: Cambridge University Press, 1920.

The Facsimile Edition of the Nag Hammadi Codices: Codex II. Published under the auspices of the Department of Antiquities of the Arab Republic of Egypt, in conjunction with UNESCO. Leiden: E. J. Brill, 1974.

Fallon, Francis T., and Ron Cameron. "The Gospel of Thomas: A Forschungsbericht and Analysis." Pp. 4195–4251 in *Aufstieg und Niedergang der römischen Welt* II.25.6. Ed. Hildegard Temporini and Wolfgang Haase. Berlin/New York: Walter de Gruyter, 1988.

Fitzmyer, Joseph A. "The Oxyrhynchus Logoi of Jesus and the Coptic Gospel According to Thomas." Pp. 355–433 in idem, *Essays on the Semitic Background of the New Testament*. London: Chapman, 1971.

Gärtner, Bertil. *The Theology of the Gospel According to Thomas*. Trans. Eric J. Sharpe. New York: Harper & Brothers, 1961.

Grant, Robert M., and David Noel Freedman. *The Secret Sayings of Jesus, with an English Translation of the Gospel of Thomas by William R. Schoedel*. Garden City, NY: Doubleday, 1960; London: Collins, 1960.

Grenfell, Bernard P., and Arthur S. Hunt. ΛΟΓΙΑ ΙΗΣΟΥ: *Sayings of Our Lord*. Egypt Exploration Fund. London: Henry Frowde, 1897.

———. *New Sayings of Jesus and Fragment of a Lost Gospel from Oxyrhynchus*. Egypt Exploration Fund. London: Henry Frowde, 1904.

Guillaumont, A. "Les sémitismes dans l'Évangile selon Thomas: Essai de classement." Pp. 190–204 in *Studies in Gnosticism and Hellenistic Religions Presented to Gilles Quispel on the Occasion of His 65th Birthday*. Ed. R. van den Broek and M. J. Vermaseren. Études préliminaires aux religions orientales dans l'empire romain 91. Leiden: E. J. Brill, 1981.

———. "Sémitismes dans les logia de Jésus retrouvés à Nag-Hamâdi." *Journal asiatique* 246 (1958): 113–23.

———, H.-Ch. Puech, G. Quispel, W. Till, and Yassah 'Abd al Masîḥ, trans. *The Gospel According to Thomas*. Leiden: E. J. Brill, 1959; New York: Harper & Row, 1959.

Haenchen, Ernst. "Die Anthropologie des Thomas-Evangeliums." Pp. 207–27 in *Neues Testament und christliche Existenz: Festschrift für Herbert Braun zum 70. Geburtstag am 4. May 1973*. Ed. Hans Dieter Betz and Luise Schottroff. Tübingen: Mohr-Siebeck, 1973.

———. *Die Botschaft des Thomas-Evangeliums*. Theologische Bibliothek Töpelmann 6. Berlin: Töpelmann, 1961.

———. "Literatur zum Thomasevangelium." *Theologische Rundschau* 27 (1961–62): 147–78, 306–38.

Hedrick, Charles W. "Thomas and the Synoptics: Aiming at a Consensus." *The Second Century* 7 (1989–90): 39–56.

Hock, Ronald F., and Edward N. O'Neil. *The Chreia in Ancient Rhetoric, Volume 1: Progymnasmata*. Society of Biblical Literature Texts and Translations 27, Graeco-Roman Religion 9. Atlanta: Scholars, 1985.

Hofius, Otfried. "Das koptische Thomasevangelium und die Oxyrhynchus-Papyri Nr. 1, 654 und 655." *Evangelische Theologie* 20 (1960): 21–42, 182–92.

Jackson, Howard M. *The Lion Becomes Man: The Gnostic Leontomorphic Creator and the Platonic Tradition*. Society of

Biblical Literature Dissertation Series 81. Atlanta: Scholars, 1985.

Jeremias, Joachim. *Unknown Sayings of Jesus*. Trans. Reginald H. Fuller. New York: Macmillan, 1957.

Kasser, Rodolphe. *L'Évangile selon Thomas: Présentation et commentaire théologique*. Bibliothèque théologique. Neuchâtel: Delachaux et Niestlé, 1961.

Kee, Howard C. "'Becoming a Child' in the Gospel of Thomas." *Journal of Biblical Literature* 82 (1963): 307–14.

Klijn, A. F. J. "The 'Single One' in the Gospel of Thomas." *Journal of Biblical Literature* 81 (1962): 271–78.

Kloppenborg, John S., Marvin W. Meyer, Stephen J. Patterson, and Michael G. Steinhauser. *Q-Thomas Reader*. Sonoma, CA: Polebridge, 1990.

Koester, Helmut. "Gnostic Sayings and Controversy Traditions in John 8:12–59." Pp. 97–110 in *Nag Hammadi, Gnosticism, and Early Christianity*. Ed. Charles W. Hedrick and Robert Hodgson, Jr. Peabody, MA: Hendrickson, 1986.

————. "Jesus the Victim." *Journal of Biblical Literature* 111 (1992): 3–15.

————. "Three Thomas Parables." Pp. 195–203 in *The New Testament and Gnosis: Essays in Honour of Robert McL. Wilson*. Ed. A. H. B. Logan and A. J. M. Wedderburn. Edinburgh: T. & T. Clark, 1983.

Layton, Bentley. *The Gnostic Scriptures: A New Translation with Annotations and Introductions*. Garden City, NY: Doubleday, 1987.

————, ed. *Nag Hammadi Codex II,2–7, Together with XIII,2*, Brit. Lib. Or. 4926(1), and P. Oxy. 1, 654, 655*. 2 vols. Nag Hammadi Studies 20–21. Leiden: E. J. Brill, 1989.

Mack, Burton L. *A Myth of Innocence: Mark and Christian Origins*. Philadelphia: Fortress, 1988.

Marcovich, M. "Textual Criticism on the Gospel of Thomas." *Journal of Theological Studies*, New Series, 20 (1969): 53–74.

Ménard, Jacques-É. *L'Évangile selon Thomas*. Nag Hammadi Studies 5. Leiden: E. J. Brill, 1975.

Meyer, Marvin W. "The Beginning of the Gospel of Thomas." Pp. 161–73 in *Semeia 52: How Gospels Begin*. Ed. Dennis E. Smith. Atlanta: Scholars, 1990.

————. "Making Mary Male: The Categories 'Male' and 'Female' in the Gospel of Thomas." *New Testament Studies* 31 (1985) 554–70.

————. *The Secret Teachings of Jesus: Four Gnostic Gospels*. New York: Random House, 1984.

————, and Stephen J. Patterson. "The Gospel of Thomas." Pp. 301–22 in *The Complete Gospels: Annotated Scholars Version*. Ed. Robert J. Miller. Sonoma, CA: Polebridge, 1992.

Mirecki, Paul A. "Coptic Manichaean Psalm 278 and Gospel of Thomas 37." Pp. 243–62 in *Manichaica Selecta: Studies Presented to Professor Julien Ries on the Occasion of His Seventieth Birthday*. Ed. Alois van Tongerloo and Søren Giversen. Manichaean Studies 1. Louvain: International Association of Manichaean Studies/Belgian Center of Manichaean Studies/Center of the History of Religions, 1991.

Neller, Kenneth V. "Diversity in the Gospel of Thomas: Clues for a New Direction?" *The Second Century* 7 (1989–90): 1–18.

Patterson, Stephen J. "The Gospel of Thomas: Introduction." Pp. 77–123 in John S. Kloppenborg, Marvin W. Meyer, Stephen J. Patterson, and Michael G. Steinhauser, *Q-Thomas Reader*. Sonoma, CA: Polebridge, 1990.

————. *The Gospel of Thomas and Jesus*. Sonoma, CA: Polebridge, 1992.

Pines, Shlomo. *The Jewish Christians of the Early Centuries of Christianity According to a New Source*. Proceedings of the Israel Academy of Sciences and Humanities, vol. 2, no. 13. Jerusalem: Israel Academy of Sciences and Humanities, 1966.

Puech, Henri-Charles. "The Gospel of Thomas." Pp. 278–307 in vol. 1 of *New Testament Apocrypha*. Ed. Edgar Hennecke and Wilhelm Schneemelcher, English translation ed. R. McL. Wilson. Philadelphia: Westminster, 1963.

————. "Un logion de Jésus sur bandelette funéraire." *Revue de l'histoire des religions* 147 (1955): 126–29.

Quispel, Gilles. *Gnostic Studies II*. Uitgaven van het Nederlands Historisch-Archaeologisch Instituut te Istanbul 34/2. Istanbul: Nederlands Historisch-Archaeologisch Instituut te Istanbul, 1975.

————. "The *Gospel of Thomas* Revisited." Pp. 218–66 in *Colloque international sur les textes de Nag Hammadi (Québec, 22–25 août 1978)*. Ed. Bernard Barc. Bibliothèque copte de Nag Hammadi, Section "Études" 1. Québec: Les presses de l'Université Laval; Louvain: Éditions Peeters, 1981.

————. *Makarius, das Thomasevangelium und das Lied von der Perle.* Novum Testamentum, Supplement 15. Leiden: E. J. Brill, 1967.

————. "The Syrian Thomas and the Syrian Macarius." Pp. 112–21 in idem, *Gnostic Studies II.*

————. *Tatian and the Gospel of Thomas: Studies in the History of the Western Diatessaron.* Leiden: E. J. Brill, 1975.

Resch, Alfred, ed. *Agrapha: Aussercanonische Schriftfragmente.* 1st ed., Texte und Untersuchungen zur Geschichte der altchristlichen Literatur, 5,4 (1889). 2nd ed., Texte und Untersuchungen zur Geschichte der altchristlichen Literatur, Neue Folge, 15, 3–4 (1906). Leipzig: J. C. Hinrichs; Darmstadt: Wissenschaftliche Buchgesellschaft, 1967.

Robinson, James M. "The Discovery of the Nag Hammadi Codices." *Biblical Archeologist* 42 (1979): 206–24.

————. "From the Cliff to Cairo: The Story of the Discoverers and the Middlemen of the Nag Hammadi Codices." Pp. 21–58 in *Colloque international sur les textes de Nag Hammadi (Québec, 22–25 août 1978)*. Ed. Bernard Barc. Bibliothèque copte de Nag Hammadi, Section "Études" 1. Québec: Les presses de l'Université Laval; Louvain: Éditions Peeters, 1981.

————. "Introduction." Pp. 1–102 in *The Facsimile Edition of the Nag Hammadi Codices: Introduction.* Published under the auspices of the Department of Antiquities of the Arab Republic of Egypt, in conjunction with UNESCO. Leiden: E. J. Brill, 1984.

————, ed. *The Nag Hammadi Library in English.* Rev. ed. San Francisco: Harper & Row, 1988.

————. "On Bridging the Gulf from Q to the Gospel of Thomas (or Vice Versa)." Pp. 127–75 in *Nag Hammadi, Gnosticism, and Early Christianity.* Ed. Charles W. Hedrick and Robert Hodgson, Jr. Peabody, MA: Hendrickson, 1986.

————, and Helmut Koester. *Trajectories through Early Christianity*. Philadelphia: Fortress, 1971.

Rosenberg, David, and Harold Bloom. *The Book of J*. New York: Grove Weidenfeld, 1990.

Rudolph, Kurt. *Gnosis: The Nature and History of Gnosticism*. Translation ed. Robert McLachlan Wilson. San Francisco: Harper & Row, 1983.

Scholer, David M. "Bibliographia Gnostica: Supplementum," *Novum Testamentum* 13 (1971): 322–36; 14 (1972): 312–31; 15 (1973): 327–45; 16 (1974): 316–36; 17 (1975): 305–36; 19 (1977): 293–336; 20 (1978): 300–331; 21 (1979): 357–82; 22 (1980): 352–84; 23 (1981): 361–80; 24 (1982): 340–68; 25 (1983): 356–81; 26 (1984): 341–73; 27 (1985): 349–78; 28 (1986): 356–80; 29 (1987): 353–81; 30 (1988): 339–72; 31 (1989): 344–78; 32 (1990): 349–73; 34 (1992): 48–89.

————. *Nag Hammadi Bibliography 1948–1969*. Nag Hammadi Studies 1. Leiden: E. J. Brill, 1971.

————. *Nag Hammadi Bibliography 1970–1991*. Nag Hammadi Studies. Leiden: E. J. Brill, forthcoming.

Schrage, Wolfhart. *Das Verhältnis des Thomas-Evangeliums zur synoptischen Tradition und zu den koptischen Evangelien-Übersetzungen. Zugleich ein Beitrag zur gnostichen Synoptikerdeutung*. Beihefte zur Zeitschrift für die neutestamentliche Wissenschaft 29. Berlin: Töpelmann, 1964.

Schweitzer, Albert. *The Quest of the Historical Jesus: A Critical Study of Its Progress from Reimarus to Wrede*. Trans. W. Montgomery. New York: Macmillan, 1968.

Smith, Jonathan Z. "The Garments of Shame." *History of Religions* 5 (1965–66): 217–38. Reprinted, pp. 1–23 in idem, *Map Is Not Territory: Studies in the History of Religions*. Studies in Judaism in Late Antiquity 23. Leiden: E. J. Brill, 1978.

Snodgrass, Klyne R. "The Gospel of Thomas: A Secondary Gospel." *The Second Century* 7 (1989–90): 19–38.

Stone, Michael E., and John Strugnell, trans. *The Books of Elijah: Parts 1–2*. Society of Biblical Literature Texts and Translations 18, Pseudepigrapha 8. Missoula, MT: Scholars, 1979.

Strack, Hermann L., and Paul Billerbeck. *Kommentar zum Neuen Testament aus Talmud und Midrasch.* 6 vols. 5th ed. München: Beck, 1969.

Stroker, William D. *Extracanonical Sayings of Jesus.* Society of Biblical Literature Resources for Biblical Study 18. Atlanta: Scholars, 1989.

Suarez, Philippe de. *L'Évangile selon Thomas: Traduction, Présentation et Commentaires.* Marsanne: Éditions Métanoïa, 1975.

Till, Walter C. "New Sayings of Jesus in the Recently Discovered Coptic 'Gospel of Thomas.'" *Bulletin of the John Rylands University Library of Manchester* 41 (1959): 446–58.

Turner, H. E. W., and Hugh Montefiore. *Thomas and the Evangelists.* Studies in Biblical Theology 35. London: SCM, 1962; Naperville: Allenson, 1962.

Vielhauer, Philipp. "ΑΝΑΠΑΥΣΙΣ: Zum gnostischen Hintergrund des Thomasevangeliums." Pp. 281–99 in *Apophoreta: Festschrift für Ernst Haenchen zu seinem siebzigsten Geburtstag am 10. Dezember 1964.* Ed. Walter Eltester and Franz Heinrich Kettler. Beihefte zur Zeitschrift für die neutestamentliche Wissenschaft 30. Berlin: Töpelmann, 1964.

Williams, Michael A. *The Immovable Race: A Gnostic Designation and the Theme of Stability in Late Antiquity.* Nag Hammadi Studies 29. Leiden: E. J. Brill, 1985.

Wilson, R. McL. *Studies in the Gospel of Thomas.* London: A. R. Mowbray, 1960.